MAX LUCADO

LIFE LESSONS *from*

MATTHEW

The Carpenter King

PREPARED BY THE LIVINGSTONE CORPORATION

THOMAS NELSON
Since 1798

Life Lessons from Matthew

© 2018 by Max Lucado

Published in Nashville, Tennessee, by Thomas Nelson. Thomas Nelson is a registered trademark of HarperCollins Christian Publishing, Inc.

Produced with the assistance of the Livingstone Corporation. Project staff include Jake Barton, Joel Bartlett, Andy Culbertson, Mary Horner Collins, Will Reaves, and Rachel Hawkins.

Editor: Len Woods

All Scripture quotations, unless otherwise indicated, are taken from *The Holy Bible, New International Version*, *NIV*. Copyright © 1973, 1978, 1984, 2011 by Biblica, Inc.™ Used by permission. All rights reserved worldwide.

Scripture quotations marked NKJV are taken from the New King James Version*. Copyright © 1982 by Thomas Nelson. Used by permission. All rights reserved.

Scripture quotations marked NCV are taken from the New Century Version*. Copyright © 1987, 1988, 1991 by Word Publishing. All rights reserved.

Scripture quotations marked NLT are taken from The Holy Bible, New Living Translation. Copyright © 1996, 2004. Used by permission of Tyndale House Publishers, Inc., Carol Stream, Illinois 60188. All rights reserved.

Material for the "Inspiration" sections taken from the following books:

And the Angels Were Silent. Copyright © 1992, 2004 by Max Lucado. Thomas Nelson, a registered trademark of HarperCollins Christian Publishing, Inc., Nashville, Tennessee.

The Applause of Heaven. Copyright © 1990, 1996, 1999 by Max Lucado. Thomas Nelson, a registered trademark of HarperCollins Christian Publishing, Inc., Nashville, Tennessee.

Because of Bethlehem. Copyright © 2016 by Max Lucado. Thomas Nelson, a registered trademark of HarperCollins Christian Publishing, Inc., Nashville, Tennessee.

Before Amen. Copyright © 2014 by Max Lucado. Thomas Nelson, a registered trademark of HarperCollins Christian Publishing, Inc., Nashville, Tennessee.

Cure for the Common Life. Copyright © 2005 by Max Lucado. Thomas Nelson, a registered trademark of HarperCollins Christian Publishing, Inc., Nashville, Tennessee.

A Gentle Thunder. Copyright © 1995 by Max Lucado. Thomas Nelson, a registered trademark of HarperCollins Christian Publishing, Inc., Nashville, Tennessee.

In the Eye of the Storm. Copyright © 1991 by Max Lucado. Thomas Nelson, a registered trademark of HarperCollins Christian Publishing, Inc., Nashville, Tennessee.

Just Like Jesus. Copyright © 1998 by Max Lucado. Thomas Nelson, a registered trademark of HarperCollins Christian Publishing, Inc., Nashville, Tennessee.

Next Door Savior. Copyright © 2003 by Max Lucado. Thomas Nelson, a registered trademark of HarperCollins Christian Publishing, Inc., Nashville, Tennessee.

Traveling Light. Copyright © 2001 by Max Lucado. Thomas Nelson, a registered trademark of HarperCollins Christian Publishing, Inc., Nashville, Tennessee.

When Christ Comes. Copyright © 1999 by Max Lucado. Thomas Nelson, a registered trademark of HarperCollins Christian Publishing, Inc., Nashville, Tennessee.

Thomas Nelson titles may be purchased in bulk for educational, business, fundraising, or sales promotional use. For information, please e-mail SpecialMarkets@ThomasNelson.com.

ISBN 978-0-310-08630-7

First Printing December 2017 / Printed in the United States of America

CONTENTS

CONTENTS

HOW TO STUDY THE BIBLE

The Bible is a peculiar book. Words crafted in another language. Deeds done in a distant era. Events recorded in a far-off land. Counsel offered to a foreign people. It is a peculiar book.

It's surprising that anyone reads it. It's too old. Some of its writings date back 5,000 years. It's too bizarre. The book speaks of incredible floods, fires, earthquakes, and people with supernatural abilities. It's too radical. The Bible calls for undying devotion to a carpenter who called himself God's Son.

Logic says this book shouldn't survive. Too old, too bizarre, too radical.

The Bible has been banned, burned, scoffed, and ridiculed. Scholars have mocked it as foolish. Kings have branded it as illegal. A thousand times over the grave has been dug and the dirge has begun, but somehow the Bible never stays in the grave. Not only has it survived, but it has also thrived. It is the single most popular book in all of history. It has been the bestselling book in the world for years!

There is no way on earth to explain it. Which perhaps is the only explanation. For the Bible's durability is not found on *earth* but in *heaven*. The millions who have tested its claims and claimed its promises know there is but one answer: the Bible is God's book and God's voice.

As you read it, you would be wise to give some thought to two questions: *What is the purpose of the Bible?* and *How do I study the Bible?* Time spent reflecting on these two issues will greatly enhance your Bible study.

What is the purpose of the Bible?

Let the Bible itself answer that question: *"From infancy you have known the Holy Scriptures, which are able to make you wise for salvation through faith in Christ Jesus"* (2 Timothy 3:15).

The purpose of the Bible? Salvation. God's highest passion is to get his children home. His book, the Bible, describes his plan of salvation. The purpose of the Bible is to proclaim God's plan and passion to save his children.

This is the reason why this book has endured through the centuries. It dares to tackle the toughest questions about life: *Where do I go after I die? Is there a God? What do I do with my fears?* The Bible is the treasure map that leads to God's highest treasure—eternal life.

But how do you study the Bible? Countless copies of Scripture sit unread on bookshelves and nightstands simply because people don't know how to read it. What can you do to make the Bible real in your life?

The clearest answer is found in the words of Jesus: *"Ask and it will be given to you; seek and you will find; knock and the door will be opened to you"* (Matthew 7:7).

The first step in understanding the Bible is asking God to help you. You should read it prayerfully. If anyone understands God's Word, it is because of God and not the reader.

"The Advocate, the Holy Spirit, whom the Father will send in my name, will teach you all things and will remind you of everything I have said to you" (John 14:26).

Before reading the Bible, pray and invite God to speak to you. Don't go to Scripture looking for your idea, but go searching for his.

Not only should you read the Bible prayerfully, but you should also read it carefully. *"Seek and you will find"* is the pledge. The Bible is not a newspaper to be skimmed but rather a mine to be quarried. *"If you look for it as for silver and search for it as for hidden treasure, then you will understand the fear of the* LORD *and find the knowledge of God"* (Proverbs 2:4–5).

Any worthy find requires effort. The Bible is no exception. To understand the Bible, you don't have to be brilliant, but you must be willing to roll up your sleeves and search.

"Do your best to present yourself to God as one approved, a worker who does not need to be ashamed and who correctly handles the word of truth" (2 Timothy 2:15).

Here's a practical point. Study the Bible a bit at a time. Hunger is not satisfied by eating twenty-one meals in one sitting once a week. The body needs a steady diet to remain strong. So does the soul. When God sent food to his people in the wilderness, he didn't provide loaves already made. Instead, he sent them manna in the shape of *"thin flakes like frost on the ground"* (Exodus 16:14).

God gave manna in limited portions.

God sends spiritual food the same way. He opens the heavens with just enough nutrients for today's hunger. He provides *"a rule for this, a rule for that; a little here, a little there"* (Isaiah 28:10).

Don't be discouraged if your reading reaps a small harvest. Some days a lesser portion is all that is needed. What is important is to search every day for that day's message. A steady diet of God's Word over a lifetime builds a healthy soul and mind.

It's much like the little girl who returned from her first day at school feeling a bit dejected. Her mom asked, "Did you learn anything?"

"Apparently not enough," the girl responded. "I have to go back tomorrow, and the next day, and the next . . ."

Such is the case with learning. And such is the case with Bible study. Understanding comes little by little over a lifetime.

There is a third step in understanding the Bible. After the asking and seeking comes the knocking. After you ask and search, *"knock and the door will be opened to you"* (Matthew 7:7).

To knock is to stand at God's door. To make yourself available. To climb the steps, cross the porch, stand at the doorway, and volunteer. Knocking goes beyond the realm of thinking and into the realm of acting.

To knock is to ask, *What can I do? How can I obey? Where can I go?*

It's one thing to know what to do. It's another to do it. But for those who do it—those who choose to obey—a special reward awaits them.

"Whoever looks intently into the perfect law that gives freedom, and continues in it—not forgetting what they have heard, but doing it—they will be blessed in what they do" (James 1:25).

What a promise. Blessings come to those who do what they read in God's Word! It's the same with medicine. If you only read the label but ignore the pills, it won't help. It's the same with food. If you only read the recipe but never cook, you won't be fed. And it's the same with the Bible. If you only read the words but never obey, you'll never know the joy God has promised.

Ask. Search. Knock. Simple, isn't it? So why don't you give it a try? If you do, you'll see why the Bible is the most remarkable book in history.

INTRODUCTION TO
The Gospel of Matthew

Yxou gotta wonder what Jesus saw in Matthew. He was a tax collector. The profession hasn't been too popular in any era, but especially not in the days of Christ. Tax collectors were the quislings of Palestine. They took from their own people and gave to Rome. As long as they met their quota, they could tax whatever they wanted and as much as they wanted.

Not only was Matthew a tax collector, but he was also a public tax collector. Some collectors did their business underground. They hired runners to do their dirty work. Matthew did his own. He was the leech at the bottom of the pit. He pulled his stretch limo right into the greasiest parts of town and set up his table and held out his hand.

That's where he was when Jesus called him.

You gotta wonder what Jesus saw in Matthew. At the same time, you gotta wonder what Matthew saw in Jesus. I mean, look at him. Dirt under his nails. Calloused hands. Holes in his sandals. No headquarters. No office. No committee. No clout with the local church.

The clergy won't give him the time of day. His followers look more like dockhands or pool sharks than seminarians.

This guy claims to be the Messiah?

Quite a pair, these two. But Matthew accepted Christ's invitation and never turned back. He spent the rest of his life convincing folks that this carpenter was the King. Jesus gave the call and never took it back. The relationship Jesus had with Matthew can serve to convince us that if Jesus had a place for Matthew, he just might have a place for us.

AUTHOR AND DATE

Matthew, also called Levi. He is first mentioned in the Gospels as being a "publican" (a tax collector for the Romans) in the town of Capernaum, where he left to follow Jesus and become one of the twelve disciples (see Matthew 9:9). He appears throughout the Gospels and was a witness of Jesus' resurrection and ascension into heaven. As a publican, Matthew would have been literate in both Aramaic and Greek. It is believed he wrote his Gospel c. AD 60.

SITUATION

Many scholars locate the writing of the Gospel in Antioch, a Greek-speaking city with a substantial Jewish population. Matthew is believed to have written for a Jewish audience, revealing through family records that Jesus was a descendant of both King David and Abraham (see Matthew 1:1–17). Matthew is distinctive in citing a number of Old Testament prophecies that Jesus fulfilled during his ministry (see, for example, Matthew 1:22; 2:15; 4:14; 8:17; 13:35; 21:4).

KEY THEMES

- God kept his promise of a deliverer for his people.
- God's ideas about his kingdom are often different from his people's ideas of the same kingdom.
- Jesus lived fully as a human and as God.
- Jesus' ministry and sacrifice changed the world forever.

KEY VERSE

Therefore go and make disciples of all nations, baptizing them in the name of the Father and of the Son and of the Holy Spirit (Matthew 28:19).

CONTENTS

LESSON ONE

GOD WITH SKIN ON

"She will bring forth a Son, and you shall call His name Jesus, for He will save His people from their sins."
MATTHEW 1:21 NKJV

REFLECTION

Each December, Christians look back on the mind-boggling events of that first Christmas—angel armies appearing to awestruck shepherds, the star of Bethlehem guiding the wise men, and, of course, the baby in the manger. What do you do each holiday season to remember and savor the stunning claim of the gospel: that God took on flesh and made his dwelling among us?

SITUATION

Writing to his fellow Jews, Matthew begins his Gospel by demonstrating how Jesus descended (humanly speaking) from both Abraham and King David. He then discusses some of the circumstances surrounding Christ's virgin birth and stormy infancy. Matthew's Gospel is unique in that it provides the only account of the wise men's visit and King Herod's murderous plot to kill all male children under the age of two in the region of Bethlehem.

OBSERVATION

Read Matthew 1:18–2:12 from the New International Version or the New King James Version.

New International Version

1:18 This is how the birth of Jesus the Messiah came about: His mother Mary was pledged to be married to Joseph, but before they came together, she was found to be pregnant through the Holy Spirit. 19 Because

Joseph her husband was faithful to the law, and yet did not want to expose her to public disgrace, he had in mind to divorce her quietly.

²⁰ But after he had considered this, an angel of the Lord appeared to him in a dream and said, "Joseph son of David, do not be afraid to take Mary home as your wife, because what is conceived in her is from the Holy Spirit. ²¹ She will give birth to a son, and you are to give him the name Jesus, because he will save his people from their sins."

²² All this took place to fulfill what the Lord had said through the prophet: ²³ "The virgin will conceive and give birth to a son, and they will call him Immanuel" (which means "God with us").

²⁴ When Joseph woke up, he did what the angel of the Lord had commanded him and took Mary home as his wife. ²⁵ But he did not consummate their marriage until she gave birth to a son. And he gave him the name Jesus.

²:¹ After Jesus was born in Bethlehem in Judea, during the time of King Herod, Magi from the east came to Jerusalem ² and asked, "Where is the one who has been born king of the Jews? We saw his star when it rose and have come to worship him."

³ When King Herod heard this he was disturbed, and all Jerusalem with him. ⁴ When he had called together all the people's chief priests and teachers of the law, he asked them where the Messiah was to be born. ⁵ "In Bethlehem in Judea," they replied, "for this is what the prophet has written:

⁶ "'But you, Bethlehem, in the land of Judah,
    are by no means least among the rulers of Judah;
        for out of you will come a ruler
        who will shepherd my people Israel.'"

⁷ Then Herod called the Magi secretly and found out from them the exact time the star had appeared. ⁸ He sent them to Bethlehem and said, "Go and search carefully for the child. As soon as you find him, report to me, so that I too may go and worship him."

⁹ After they had heard the king, they went on their way, and the star they had seen when it rose went ahead of them until it stopped over the place where the child was. ¹⁰ When they saw the star, they were over-joyed. ¹¹ On coming to the house, they saw the child with his mother Mary, and they bowed down and worshiped him. Then they opened their treasures and presented him with gifts of gold, frankincense and myrrh. ¹² And having been warned in a dream not to go back to Herod, they returned to their country by another route.

NEW KING JAMES VERSION

¹:¹⁸ Now the birth of Jesus Christ was as follows: After His mother Mary was betrothed to Joseph, before they came together, she was found with child of the Holy Spirit. ¹⁹ Then Joseph her husband, being a just man, and not wanting to make her a public example, was minded to put her away secretly. ²⁰ But while he thought about these things, behold, an angel of the Lord appeared to him in a dream, saying, "Joseph, son of David, do not be afraid to take to you Mary your wife, for that which is conceived in her is of the Holy Spirit. ²¹ And she will bring forth a Son, and you shall call His name Jesus, for He will save His people from their sins."

²² So all this was done that it might be fulfilled which was spoken by the Lord through the prophet, saying: ²³ "Behold, the virgin shall be with child, and bear a Son, and they shall call His name Immanuel," which is translated, "God with us."

²⁴ Then Joseph, being aroused from sleep, did as the angel of the Lord commanded him and took to him his wife, ²⁵ and did not know her till she had brought forth her firstborn Son. And he called His name Jesus.

²:¹ Now after Jesus was born in Bethlehem of Judea in the days of Herod the king, behold, wise men from the East came to Jerusalem, ² saying, "Where is He who has been born King of the Jews? For we have seen His star in the East and have come to worship Him."

³ When Herod the king heard this, he was troubled, and all Jerusalem with him. ⁴ And when he had gathered all the chief priests and scribes of the people together, he inquired of them where the Christ was to be born.

⁵ So they said to him, "In Bethlehem of Judea, for thus it is written by the prophet:

> ⁶ 'But you, Bethlehem, in the land of Judah,
> Are not the least among the rulers of Judah;
> For out of you shall come a Ruler
> Who will shepherd My people Israel.'"

⁷ Then Herod, when he had secretly called the wise men, determined from them what time the star appeared. ⁸ And he sent them to Bethlehem and said, "Go and search carefully for the young Child, and when you have found Him, bring back word to me, that I may come and worship Him also."

⁹ When they heard the king, they departed; and behold, the star which they had seen in the East went before them, till it came and stood over where the young Child was. ¹⁰ When they saw the star, they rejoiced with exceedingly great joy. ¹¹ And when they had come into the house, they saw the young Child with Mary His mother, and fell down and worshiped Him. And when they had opened their treasures, they presented gifts to Him: gold, frankincense, and myrrh.

¹² Then, being divinely warned in a dream that they should not return to Herod, they departed for their own country another way.

EXPLORATION

1. Why would Christ's ancestry have mattered to the Jewish readers of Matthew's Gospel?

_____

_____

_____

_____

2. It is often said that "things are not what they seem to be." How does this statement apply to Mary's pregnancy and the coming of Christ into the world?

3. What can we learn about Joseph's character from Matthew 1–2?

4. What was Herod's response to the news that Christ, "the king of the Jews," had come?

5. Why do you think wise men from the East traveled so far and so long to find Christ, while Israel's religious scholars and leaders didn't look for him at all?

6. How did the wise men locate Jesus? What did they do when they finally found him?

INSPIRATION

People have always wondered about the image of God. Societies have speculated. Tribes have cogitated. And we've reached a variety of conclusions. God has been depicted as a golden calf and a violent wind and an angry volcano. He wears wings, breathes fire, eats infants, and demands penance. We've fancied God as ferocious, magical, fickle, and maniacal. A god to be avoided, dreaded, and appeased. But never in mankind's wildest imaginings did we consider that God would enter the world as an infant.

"The Word became flesh and dwelt among us" (John 1:14 NKJV). The Word became not a whirlwind or a devouring fire but a single cell, a fertilized egg, an embryo—a baby. Placenta nourished him. An amniotic sac surrounded him. He grew to the size of a fist. His tiny heart divided into chambers. God became flesh.

Jesus entered our world not *like* a human but *as* a human. He endured puberty, pimples, hot weather, and cranky neighbors. God became human down to his very toes. He had suspended the stars and ladled out the seas, yet he suckled a breast and slept in hay. . . .

Why such a journey? Why did God go so far?

A chief reason is this: *he wants you to know that he gets you.* He understands how you feel and has faced what you face. Jesus is not "out of touch with our reality. He's been through weakness and testing, experienced it all—all but the sin. So let's walk right up to him and get what he is so ready to give. Take the mercy, accept the help" (Hebrews 4:15–16 MSG).

Since you know he understands, you can boldly go to him. Because of Bethlehem's miracle, you can answer these fundamental questions: *Does God care if I'm sad?* Look at the tear-streaked face of Jesus as he stands near Lazarus's tomb. *Does God notice when I'm afraid?* Note the resolve in the eyes of Jesus as he marches through the storm to rescue his friends. *Does God know if I am ignored or rejected?* Find the answer in the compassionate eyes of Christ as he stands to defend the adulterous woman. . . .

Gaze where Mary gazed. Look into God's face and be assured. If the King was willing to enter the world of animals and shepherds and swaddling clothes, don't you think he's willing to enter yours? He took on your face in the hope that you would see his. (From *Because of Bethlehem* by Max Lucado.)

REACTION

7. How do you respond to the biblical claim that for three decades, the Creator of heaven and earth actually moved into the midst of his creation?

_____

_____

_____

_____

8. Why do you think it is difficult for some to grasp that Jesus is God incarnate?

_____

_____

_____

_____

9. When has God seemed the most real, the most tangible, and the most near to you?

_____

_____

_____

_____

10. What lessons can you learn from Joseph about submitting to the big purposes of God?

_____

_____

_____

_____

11. How do the wise men on the one hand and King Herod on the other represent the two divergent responses most people have to Christ?

12. The wise men gave so much to Christ—their attention, time, energy, effort, affection, worship, and wealth. They risked their lives, and perhaps also their careers, credibility, and reputations. Take a moment to assess your life and your devotion to Christ. Right now, what specifically are you giving him?

LIFE LESSONS

If we ever doubt God's love for us, we need look no further than the child of Bethlehem. That's no mere infant lying there in the feeding trough—he's Deity in diapers. The universe watched with wonder as heaven's (and earth's) King learned to walk. Jesus would grow up in a Jewish home. For thirty-three years he would feel everything you and I have ever felt. Weakness. Weariness. Fear of failure. Temptation. Fully human, we can safely assume Christ got colds and that he stumped his toes. His feelings got hurt. His feet got tired. And his head ached. To think of Jesus in such a light is—well, it seems almost irreverent, doesn't it? It's not something we like to do; it's uncomfortable. It is much easier to keep the humanity out of the incarnation. But it's also unbiblical. Christ was God . . . with skin on.

DEVOTION

Father, thank you for sending your Son to be with us and to die for us. Jesus, thank you for being our personal Savior. Spirit of God, open our eyes to the wondrous truth of the gospel. May we daily be amazed by your grace. May we walk in your power. May we have courage and joy to share the good news of Immanuel, God with us.

JOURNALING

How would your life tomorrow be different if you could continually live with an awareness that Christ is with you and in you?

_____

_____

_____

_____

_____

_____

_____

FOR FURTHER READING

To complete the book of Matthew during this twelve-part study, read Matthew 1:1–2:23. For more Bible passages on the Incarnation, read Isaiah 7:14; Luke 1:26–2:21; and John 1:1–18.

LESSON TWO

OVERCOMING TEMPTATION

Jesus said to him, "Away from me, Satan! For it is written:
'Worship the Lord your God, and serve him only.'"
MATTHEW 4:10

REFLECTION

Even more certain than death, hunger, and taxes is the reality of temptation. And worse, as someone once quipped, temptations are like stray cats—treat one nicely, and before you can blink, it will be back with a dozen of its friends! How would you define temptation to a child? How would you describe the process of being lured into sin?

_____

_____

_____

_____

SITUATION

Matthew, like the other Gospel writers, wastes little time in getting to the beginning of Christ's public ministry. After relating the story of Jesus' birth, he quickly moves to describing the Lord's baptism and his temptation in the wilderness. These events serve as the starting point in each of the Gospels for Jesus' subsequent ministry on earth.

OBSERVATION

Read Matthew 3:13–4:11 from the New International Version or the New King James Version.

NEW INTERNATIONAL VERSION

3:13 Then Jesus came from Galilee to the Jordan to be baptized by John. 14 But John tried to deter him, saying, "I need to be baptized by you, and do you come to me?"

15 Jesus replied, "Let it be so now; it is proper for us to do this to fulfill all righteousness." Then John consented.

[16] As soon as Jesus was baptized, he went up out of the water. At that moment heaven was opened, and he saw the Spirit of God descending like a dove and alighting on him. [17] And a voice from heaven said, "This is my Son, whom I love; with him I am well pleased."

[4:1] Then Jesus was led by the Spirit into the wilderness to be tempted by the devil. [2] After fasting forty days and forty nights, he was hungry. [3] The tempter came to him and said, "If you are the Son of God, tell these stones to become bread."

[4] Jesus answered, "It is written: 'Man shall not live on bread alone, but on every word that comes from the mouth of God.'"

[5] Then the devil took him to the holy city and had him stand on the highest point of the temple. [6] "If you are the Son of God," he said, "throw yourself down. For it is written:

> "'He will command his angels concerning you
> and they will lift you up in their hands,
> so that you will not strike your foot against a stone.'"

[7] Jesus answered him, "It is also written: 'Do not put the Lord your God to the test.'"

[8] Again, the devil took him to a very high mountain and showed him all the kingdoms of the world and their splendor. [9] "All this I will give you," he said, "if you will bow down and worship me."

[10] Jesus said to him, "Away from me, Satan! For it is written: 'Worship the Lord your God, and serve him only.'"

[11] Then the devil left him, and angels came and attended him.

NEW KING JAMES VERSION

[3:13] Then Jesus came from Galilee to John at the Jordan to be baptized by him. [14] And John tried to prevent Him, saying, "I need to be baptized by You, and are You coming to me?"

[15] But Jesus answered and said to him, "Permit it to be so now, for thus it is fitting for us to fulfill all righteousness." Then he allowed Him.

[16] When He had been baptized, Jesus came up immediately from the water; and behold, the heavens were opened to Him, and He saw the Spirit of God descending like a dove and alighting upon Him. [17] And suddenly a voice came from heaven, saying, "This is My beloved Son, in whom I am well pleased."

[4:1] Then Jesus was led up by the Spirit into the wilderness to be tempted by the devil. [2] And when He had fasted forty days and forty nights, afterward He was hungry. [3] Now when the tempter came to Him, he said, "If You are the Son of God, command that these stones become bread."

[4] But He answered and said, "It is written, 'Man shall not live by bread alone, but by every word that proceeds from the mouth of God.'"

[5] Then the devil took Him up into the holy city, set Him on the pinnacle of the temple, [6] and said to Him, "If You are the Son of God, throw Yourself down. For it is written:

'He shall give His angels charge over you,'

and,

'In their hands they shall bear you up,
Lest you dash your foot against a stone.'"

[7] Jesus said to him, "It is written again, 'You shall not tempt the Lord your God.'"

[8] Again, the devil took Him up on an exceedingly high mountain, and showed Him all the kingdoms of the world and their glory. [9] And he said to Him, "All these things I will give You if You will fall down and worship me."

[10] Then Jesus said to him, "Away with you, Satan! For it is written, 'You shall worship the Lord your God, and Him only you shall serve.'"

[11] Then the devil left Him, and behold, angels came and ministered to Him.

EXPLORATION

1. Take a few moments to look at this passage you've just read. What was John the Baptist's role in the ministry of Christ?

2. Look carefully at the sequence of events this passage. Why do you think Jesus was led into the wilderness to be tempted right after God expressed how pleased he was with him?

3. Eating food is certainly not a sin, and we know that Jesus was hungry in the wilderness. What would have been so wrong with him turning stones into bread?

4. What was Satan attempting to get Jesus to "prove" through his second temptation (see Matthew 4:5–6)? Why did Jesus refuse to take Satan up on this offer?

5. What do you think Jesus felt in the midst of this time of testing? How does this differ with how he responded?

6. How did the devil misuse Scripture to try to entice Jesus to act independently of the Father?

INSPIRATION

Have you ever thought about the evil things done to Christ? Can you think of times when Jesus could have given up? How about his time of temptation? You and I know what it is like to endure a moment of temptation or an hour of temptation, even a day of temptation. But *forty* days? That is what Jesus faced. "Jesus, full of the Holy Spirit, left the Jordan and was led by the Spirit into the wilderness, where for forty days he was tempted by the devil" (Luke 4:1–2).

We imagine the wilderness temptation as three isolated events scattered over a forty-day period. Would that it had been. In reality, Jesus' time of testing was nonstop: "for forty days he was tempted by the devil." Satan got on Jesus like a shirt and refused to leave. Every step, whispering in his ear. Every turn of the path, sowing doubt.

Was Jesus affected by the devil? Apparently so. Matthew doesn't say that Satan *tried* to tempt Jesus. The verse doesn't read, "for forty days the devil *attempted* to tempt Jesus." No, the passage is clear: "he *was tempted* by the devil." Jesus was *tempted*, he was *tested*. Tempted to change sides? Tempted to go home? Tempted to settle for a kingdom on earth? I don't know, but I know he was tempted. A war raged within. Stress stormed without. And since he was tempted, he could have quit the race. But he didn't. He kept on running.

Temptation didn't stop him, nor did accusations. Can you imagine what it would be like to run in a race and be criticized by the bystanders?

Some years ago I entered a 5K race. Nothing serious, just a jog through the neighborhood to raise funds for a charity. Not being the wisest of runners, I started off at an impossible pace. Within a mile I was sucking air. At the right time, however, the spectators encouraged me. Sympathetic onlookers urged me on. One compassionate lady passed out cups of water, another sprayed us down with a hose. I had never seen these people, but that didn't matter. I needed a voice of encouragement, and they gave it. Bolstered by their assurance, I kept going.

What if, in the toughest steps of the race, I had heard words of accusation and not encouragement? And what if the accusations came not from strangers I could dismiss but from my neighbors and family?

How would you like somebody to yell these words at you as you ran: "Hey, liar! Why don't you do something honest with your life?" (see John 7:12). "Here comes the foreigner. Why don't you go home where you belong?" (see John 8:48). "Since when do they let children of the devil enter the race?" (see John 8:48).

That's what happened to Jesus. His own family called him a lunatic. His neighbors treated him even worse. When Jesus returned to his hometown, they tried to throw him off a cliff (see Luke 4:29). But Jesus didn't quit running. Temptations didn't deter him. Accusations didn't defeat him. Nor did shame dishearten him. (From *Just Like Jesus* by Max Lucado.)

REACTION

7. Why do you think it was necessary for Jesus to be baptized before starting his ministry?

8. Why do you think John was so reluctant to baptize Jesus? What did he recognize in Christ?

9. Which of the temptations that Jesus faced would have been the most difficult for you to resist? Why?

10. Theologians like to argue about whether Christ could have actually given in to the devil's temptations. Some argue that Jesus was divine, and God is incapable of evil. Others say if it was impossible for him to give in, then this temptation account is meaningless. What do you say?

11. What are some times in your life in which you find yourself more susceptible and vulnerable to temptation than normal?

12. What have you learned from Jesus' example on how to handle temptations? What have you learned from his example about the importance of knowing God's Word?

LIFE LESSONS

We can find great comfort in Matthew's account of Christ's temptation. Theological possibilities aside, the fact remains that in Jesus' humanity, he was ravenous and exhausted, and the devil slyly moved in to try to exploit his vulnerable condition. Nothing in the text suggests Satan's wilderness attack was quick—rather, it was tricky and relentless. But Christ resisted, which means we have a victorious Savior who *truly understands* what it is like to be wooed and enticed to do evil. And in the Lord's dogged adherence to God's truth, we have a magnificent example for what to do when we find ourselves "wanting to please our sinful selves, wanting the sinful things we see, and being too proud of what we have" (1 John 2:16 NCV).

DEVOTION

Thank you, Lord, that you understand our weaknesses. While on earth, you were tempted in every way that we are. Thank you, Lord, for your steadfast refusal to sin. You are holy, and you have promised to make us holy. Grant us discernment today to do your will.

JOURNALING

What are some practical and specific steps you can take to combat the most common temptation in your life right now?

FOR FURTHER READING

To complete the book of Matthew during this twelve-part study, read Matthew 3:1–4:25. For more Bible passages on temptation, read 1 Corinthians 10:13; Hebrews 4:14–16; and James 1:12–15.

LESSON THREE

POWER IN PRAYER

*"But you, when you pray, go into your room,
and when you have shut your door, pray to your
Father who is in the secret place; and your Father
who sees in secret will reward you openly."*
MATTHEW 6:6 NKJV

REFLECTION

A major news magazine once reported that roughly four out of five adults say they pray at least once a week. The survey also revealed that eighty-five percent of those who pray claim they do *not* regularly receive answers to their prayers. How do you explain this contrast?

SITUATION

Matthew, having introduced Jesus as the long-awaited Messiah-King sent by God, relates how Jesus began his ministry by calling his first disciples and healing many people. Great multitudes began to follow him, so Jesus went up on a mountain to teach them. In this famous "Sermon on the Mount," Jesus set forth the standards of living in God's kingdom. The ability to pray effectively is among the God-honoring practices expected of those who follow Christ.

OBSERVATION

Read Matthew 6:5–15 from the New International Version or the New King James Version.

NEW INTERNATIONAL VERSION

5 "And when you pray, do not be like the hypocrites, for they love to pray standing in the synagogues and on the street corners to be seen by others. Truly I tell you, they have received their reward in full. 6 But when you

pray, go into your room, close the door and pray to your Father, who is unseen. Then your Father, who sees what is done in secret, will reward you. [7] And when you pray, do not keep on babbling like pagans, for they think they will be heard because of their many words. [8] Do not be like them, for your Father knows what you need before you ask him.

[9] "This, then, is how you should pray:

"'Our Father in heaven,
hallowed be your name,
[10] your kingdom come,
your will be done,
on earth as it is in heaven.
[11] Give us today our daily bread.
[12] And forgive us our debts,
as we also have forgiven our debtors.
[13] And lead us not into temptation,
but deliver us from the evil one.'

[14] For if you forgive other people when they sin against you, your heavenly Father will also forgive you. [15] But if you do not forgive others their sins, your Father will not forgive your sins.

NEW KING JAMES VERSION

[5] "And when you pray, you shall not be like the hypocrites. For they love to pray standing in the synagogues and on the corners of the streets, that they may be seen by men. Assuredly, I say to you, they have their reward. [6] But you, when you pray, go into your room, and when you have shut your door, pray to your Father who is in the secret place; and your Father who sees in secret will reward you openly. [7] And when you pray, do not use vain repetitions as the heathen do. For they think that they will be heard for their many words.

[8] "Therefore do not be like them. For your Father knows the things you have need of before you ask Him. [9] In this manner, therefore, pray:

Our Father in heaven,

Hallowed be Your name.

[10] Your kingdom come.

Your will be done

On earth as it is in heaven.

[11] Give us this day our daily bread.

[12] And forgive us our debts,

As we forgive our debtors.

[13] And do not lead us into temptation,

But deliver us from the evil one.

For Yours is the kingdom and the power and the glory forever.

Amen.

[14] "For if you forgive men their trespasses, your heavenly Father will also forgive you. [15] But if you do not forgive men their trespasses, neither will your Father forgive your trespasses.

EXPLORATION

1. How did Jesus describe the prayer habits of the religious "hypocrites"?

_____

_____

_____

_____

2. Why do you think Jesus instructed his followers to "close the door" when they pray? What does this tell us our attitude should be when we come before God?

_____

_____

_____

_____

3. What did Jesus say about repetitive or "wordy" prayers?

_____

_____

_____

4. Why did Jesus instruct his followers to address God as Father and not with some other title or form of address?

_____

_____

_____

5. What kind of things did Jesus command us to express before asking God to provides for our needs and desires?

_____

_____

_____

6. How is a forgiving spirit connected to effective praying?

_____

_____

_____

INSPIRATION

We might as well admit it. Prayer is odd, peculiar. Speaking into space. Lifting words into the sky. We can't even get the cable company to answer us, yet God will? The doctor is too busy, but God isn't? We have our doubts about prayer.

And we have our checkered history with prayer: unmet expectations, unanswered requests. We can barely genuflect for the scar tissue on our knees. God, to some, is the ultimate heartbreaker. Why keep tossing the coins of our longings into a silent pool? He jilted me once . . . but not twice.

Oh, the peculiar puzzle of prayer.

We aren't the first to struggle. The sign-up sheet for Prayer 101 contains some familiar names: the apostles John, James, Andrew, and Peter. When one of Jesus' disciples requested, "Lord, teach us to pray" (Luke 11:1), none of the others objected. No one walked away saying, "Hey, I have prayer figured out." The first followers of Jesus needed prayer guidance.

In fact, the only tutorial they ever requested was on prayer. They could have asked for instructions on many topics: bread multiplying, speech making, storm stilling. Jesus raised people from the dead. But a "How to Vacate the Cemetery" seminar? His followers never called for one. But they did want him to do this: "Lord, teach us to pray."

Might their interest have had something to do with the jaw-dropping, eye-popping promises Jesus attached to prayer? "Ask and it will be given to you" (Matthew 7:7). "If you believe, you will get anything you ask for in prayer" (Matthew 21:22 NCV). Jesus never attached such power to other endeavors. "*Plan* and it will be given to you." "You will get anything you *work* for." Those words are not in the Bible. But these are—"If you remain in me and follow my teachings, you can ask anything you want, and it will be given to you" (John 15:7 NCV). . . .

Do you think the disciples made the prayer–power connection? "Lord, teach us to pray *like that*. Teach us to find strength in prayer. To banish fear in prayer. To defy storms in prayer. To come off the mountain of prayer with the authority of a prince."

What about you? The disciples faced angry waves and a watery grave. You face angry clients, a turbulent economy, raging seas of stress and sorrow. "Lord," we still request, "teach us to pray." (From *Before Amen* by Max Lucado.)

REACTION

7. What are your feelings toward prayer? What would you say are some of your greatest impediments to having a more consistent prayer life?

8. Jesus observed that much of prayer is inauthentic and only for show. How much "bogus" praying goes on in churches? In your life?

9. Look again at the specific sequence of prayer Jesus advocated in Matthew 6:5–15. What is significant about this more God-centered way of praying?

10. Passages such as Mark 1:35 and Luke 6:12 give us a window into Christ's personal discipline of prayer. What are the implications for you based on Christ's example?

11. What other factors make your prayers effective? (See Luke 18:1–8 for one example.)

_____

_____

_____

12. Do you find you easily get distracted when you pray? Why do you think that is?

_____

_____

_____

LIFE LESSONS

Countless Christians have been strengthened in the area of prayer by following the A-C-T-S acronym. You begin with *Adoration*, in which you spend a few moments focusing on the nature of God (his holiness, power, mercy, goodness) and praising him for who he is. This is followed by *Confession*, where you through the help of the Spirit, acknowledge personal failings (see 1 John 1:9) and claim the endless forgiveness of God. Next comes *Thanksgiving*, in which you express appreciation and gratitude for all of God's blessings. You conclude with *Supplication*, or asking God to supply your needs and the needs of others (for power, endurance, wisdom, financial and relational help, and so on). Try this for the next few days during your commute, exercise, or other activities in your daily routine.

DEVOTION

Lord, give me a heart that hungers for you. I ask the same thing your original disciples asked, "Teach me to pray"—in faith, with boldness, and in accordance with your perfect will. Help me to see prayer not as a dry duty, but as an opportunity to commune with you, all day, every day.

JOURNALING

What are five God-honoring things you would like to see the Lord do (1) in your heart/life, (2) in your marriage/family, (3) in your church, (4) at work, and (5) in the world?

29

FOR FURTHER READING

To complete the book of Matthew during this twelve-part study, read Matthew 5:1–7:29. For more Bible passages on prayer, read Nehemiah 1:4–11; John 17:1–26; Ephesians 6:18; and Philippians 4:6–7.

LESSON FOUR

THE COMPASSION OF CHRIST

*When he saw the crowds, he had compassion
on them, because they were harassed and
helpless, like sheep without a shepherd.*
MATTHEW 9:36

REFLECTION

In her memoir *Traveling Mercies*, author Anne Lamott describes the man who was instrumental in her conversion by saying, "He was about the first Christian I ever met whom I could stand to be in the same room with. Most Christians seemed almost hostile in their belief that they were saved and you weren't." Why do you think so many non-believers feel this way about the church and about Christians?

SITUATION

Having focused on Christ's words in the Sermon on the Mount, Matthew now shines his spotlight on Christ's works. He reveals how Jesus consistently displays his divine compassion by performing miracles and relentlessly ministering to empty and hurting people. Jesus' acts of mercy only serve to accentuate the heartless indifference that Israel's religious leaders are showing toward the plight of the people.

OBSERVATION

Read Matthew 9:18–38 from the New International Version or the New King James Version.

NEW INTERNATIONAL VERSION

[18] While he was saying this, a synagogue leader came and knelt before him and said, "My daughter has just died. But come and put your hand

on her, and she will live." [19] Jesus got up and went with him, and so did his disciples.

[20] Just then a woman who had been subject to bleeding for twelve years came up behind him and touched the edge of his cloak. [21] She said to herself, "If I only touch his cloak, I will be healed."

[22] Jesus turned and saw her. "Take heart, daughter," he said, "your faith has healed you." And the woman was healed at that moment.

[23] When Jesus entered the synagogue leader's house and saw the noisy crowd and people playing pipes, [24] he said, "Go away. The girl is not dead but asleep." But they laughed at him. [25] After the crowd had been put outside, he went in and took the girl by the hand, and she got up. [26] News of this spread through all that region.

[27] As Jesus went on from there, two blind men followed him, calling out, "Have mercy on us, Son of David!"

[28] When he had gone indoors, the blind men came to him, and he asked them, "Do you believe that I am able to do this?"

"Yes, Lord," they replied.

[29] Then he touched their eyes and said, "According to your faith let it be done to you"; [30] and their sight was restored. Jesus warned them sternly, "See that no one knows about this." [31] But they went out and spread the news about him all over that region.

[32] While they were going out, a man who was demon-possessed and could not talk was brought to Jesus. [33] And when the demon was driven out, the man who had been mute spoke. The crowd was amazed and said, "Nothing like this has ever been seen in Israel."

[34] But the Pharisees said, "It is by the prince of demons that he drives out demons."

[35] Jesus went through all the towns and villages, teaching in their synagogues, proclaiming the good news of the kingdom and healing every disease and sickness. [36] When he saw the crowds, he had compassion on them, because they were harassed and helpless, like sheep without a shepherd. [37] Then he said to his disciples, "The harvest is plentiful but the workers are few. [38] Ask the Lord of the harvest, therefore, to send out workers into his harvest field."

New King James Version

¹⁸ While He spoke these things to them, behold, a ruler came and worshiped Him, saying, "My daughter has just died, but come and lay Your hand on her and she will live." ¹⁹ So Jesus arose and followed him, and so did His disciples.

²⁰ And suddenly, a woman who had a flow of blood for twelve years came from behind and touched the hem of His garment. ²¹ For she said to herself, "If only I may touch His garment, I shall be made well." ²² But Jesus turned around, and when He saw her He said, "Be of good cheer, daughter; your faith has made you well." And the woman was made well from that hour.

²³ When Jesus came into the ruler's house, and saw the flute players and the noisy crowd wailing, ²⁴ He said to them, "Make room, for the girl is not dead, but sleeping." And they ridiculed Him. ²⁵ But when the crowd was put outside, He went in and took her by the hand, and the girl arose. ²⁶ And the report of this went out into all that land.

²⁷ When Jesus departed from there, two blind men followed Him, crying out and saying, "Son of David, have mercy on us!"

²⁸ And when He had come into the house, the blind men came to Him. And Jesus said to them, "Do you believe that I am able to do this?"

They said to Him, "Yes, Lord."

²⁹ Then He touched their eyes, saying, "According to your faith let it be to you." ³⁰ And their eyes were opened. And Jesus sternly warned them, saying, "See that no one knows it." ³¹ But when they had departed, they spread the news about Him in all that country.

³² As they went out, behold, they brought to Him a man, mute and demon-possessed. ³³ And when the demon was cast out, the mute spoke. And the multitudes marveled, saying, "It was never seen like this in Israel!"

³⁴ But the Pharisees said, "He casts out demons by the ruler of the demons."

³⁵ Then Jesus went about all the cities and villages, teaching in their synagogues, preaching the gospel of the kingdom, and healing every sickness and every disease among the people. ³⁶ But when He saw the multitudes, He

was moved with compassion for them, because they were weary and scattered, like sheep having no shepherd. [37] Then He said to His disciples, "The harvest truly is plentiful, but the laborers are few. [38] Therefore pray the Lord of the harvest to send out laborers into His harvest."

EXPLORATION

1. What were the miracles in this passage that Jesus performed in rapid-fire succession?

_____

_____

_____

2. What role did faith play in these people's experiences of Christ's power?

_____

_____

3. What unusual or surprising command did Jesus give to the blind men whom he healed? Why did they disobey?

_____

_____

4. How does the "official" response of Israel's religious leaders to Christ's healing ministry compare to the response of the masses?

_____

5. What specific factors does Matthew say elicited Christ's compassion?

_____

_____

6. What did Jesus mean when he said to the disciples, "The harvest is plentiful but the workers are few" (verse 37)? What was he instructing them to do?

_____

_____

INSPIRATION

"When Jesus landed and saw a large crowd, he had compassion on them, because they were like sheep without a shepherd. So he began teaching them many things" (Mark 6:34). "When Jesus landed and saw a large crowd, he had compassion on them and healed their sick" (Matthew 14:14). It's a good thing those verses weren't written about me.

It's a good thing thousands of people weren't depending on Max for their teaching and nourishment. Especially on a day when I'd just heard of the death of a dear friend . . . especially after I'd gotten into a boat to escape the crowds. Had that been me in Jesus' sandals on that Bethsaida beach, the verses would read something like:

"They were like sheep without a shepherd. So Max told them to quit grazing on his pasture and to head back to their pens." "When Max landed and saw a large crowd, he mumbled something about how hard it was to get a day off and radioed for the helicopter. Then he and the disciples escaped to a private retreat."

It's a good thing I wasn't responsible for those people. I would have been in no mood to teach them, no mood to help them. I would have had no desire even to be with them. But, as I think about it, Jesus had no desire to be with them either. . . .

What made him change his mind and spend the day with the people he was trying to avoid? Answer? Take a look at five words in Matthew 14:14: "He had compassion on them."

The Greek word used for compassion in this passage is *splanchnizomai*, which won't mean much to you unless you are in the health professions and studied "splanchnology" in school. If so, you remember that "splanchnology" is a study of the visceral parts. Or, in contemporary jargon, a study of the gut.

When Matthew writes that Jesus had compassion on the people, he is not saying that Jesus felt casual pity for them. No, the term is far more graphic. Matthew is saying that Jesus felt their hurt in his gut:

- He felt the limp of the crippled.
- He felt the hurt of the diseased.
- He felt the loneliness of the leper.
- He felt the embarrassment of the sinful.

And once he felt their hurts, he couldn't help but heal their hurts. He was moved in the stomach by their needs. He was so touched by their needs that he forgot his own needs. (From *In the Eye of the Storm* by Max Lucado.)

REACTION

7. How would you define *compassion* in your own words?

_____

_____

8. What does the series of incidents in Matthew 9:18–38 reveal about the heart of Jesus?

9. The picture all of the Gospels paint of the Pharisees, scribes, and teachers of the law is of a dour and disapproving bunch. What do you think prompts such a petty response in the face of God's mercy and grace?

10. What are some specific things the Church could do to correct its reputation for being harsh and hostile?

11. When was the last time you felt torn up inside over the plight of someone else? What did you do?

12. How does a Christian become more compassionate? Is it actually possible to develop this quality—or is this more an issue of one's temperament? Explain.

LIFE LESSONS

The clear testimony of Scripture, both Old and New Testaments, is that God aches when his people hurt (see Exodus 2:23–25). He enters into our suffering and identifies fully with us in our pain. But more than just experiencing emotions of pity and sorrow, God is compelled by his compassion and acts (see Exodus 3:1–10). There is no better demonstration of this than

Christ. His whole ministry reveals this deep concern in the heart of God that relentlessly goes to any length to bring comfort. As followers of Jesus, as those engaged in the lifelong process of becoming like him, we must demonstrate this same kind of active compassion in an ever-increasing way.

DEVOTION

Lord Jesus, your heart overflows with an aching desire to help those who hurt. Thank you for loving me with such deep tenderness. Show me how to be more caring and compassionate in my daily life. May your gentle concern flow through me. May I be a healing presence to those around me.

JOURNALING

Who are the top candidates in your life for God's compassion today? List them and, while listening to the Spirit, brainstorm some specific steps you could take to show Christlike concern.

FOR FURTHER READING

To complete the book of Matthew during this twelve-part study, read Matthew 8:1–9:38. For more Bible passages on compassion, read Psalm 103; Psalm 116:5; Isaiah 49:13; Luke 15:20; and Colossians 3:12.

LESSON FIVE

FOLLOWING CHRIST

Whoever does not take up their cross and follow me is not worthy of me. Whoever finds their life will lose it, and whoever loses their life for my sake will find it.
MATTHEW 10:38–39 NKJV

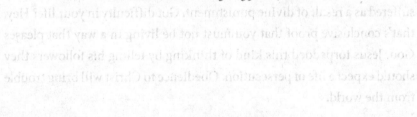

REFLECTION

The so-called health-and-wealth gospel says that because Christians are the "King's kids," we are entitled to a life of abundance and blessing. If we'll just live by faith, we will be immune from disaster and distress. We will experience favor from both God and men. What do you think about such "prosperity" teaching? Is it biblical? Why or why not?

SITUATION

Conventional wisdom during the time of Christ said that people only suffered as a result of divine punishment. Got difficulty in your life? Hey, that's conclusive proof that you must not be living in a way that pleases God. Jesus torpedoed this kind of thinking by telling his followers they should expect a life of persecution. Obedience to Christ will bring trouble from the world.

OBSERVATION

Read Matthew 10:24–42 from the New International Version or the New King James Version.

New International Version
24 "The student is not above the teacher, nor a servant above his master. 25 It is enough for students to be like their teachers, and servants like

their masters. If the head of the house has been called Beelzebul, how much more the members of his household!

26 "So do not be afraid of them, for there is nothing concealed that will not be disclosed, or hidden that will not be made known. 27 What I tell you in the dark, speak in the daylight; what is whispered in your ear, proclaim from the roofs. 28 Do not be afraid of those who kill the body but cannot kill the soul. Rather, be afraid of the One who can destroy both soul and body in hell. 29 Are not two sparrows sold for a penny? Yet not one of them will fall to the ground outside your Father's care. 30 And even the very hairs of your head are all numbered. 31 So don't be afraid; you are worth more than many sparrows.

32 "Whoever acknowledges me before others, I will also acknowledge before my Father in heaven. 33 But whoever disowns me before others, I will disown before my Father in heaven.

34 "Do not suppose that I have come to bring peace to the earth. I did not come to bring peace, but a sword. 35 For I have come to turn

"'a man against his father,
        a daughter against her mother,
    a daughter-in-law against her mother-in-law—
        36 a man's enemies will be the members of his own household.'

37 "Anyone who loves their father or mother more than me is not worthy of me; anyone who loves their son or daughter more than me is not worthy of me. 38 Whoever does not take up their cross and follow me is not worthy of me. 39 Whoever finds their life will lose it, and whoever loses their life for my sake will find it.

40 "Anyone who welcomes you welcomes me, and anyone who welcomes me welcomes the one who sent me. 41 Whoever welcomes a prophet as a prophet will receive a prophet's reward, and whoever welcomes a righteous person as a righteous person will receive a righteous person's reward. 42 And if anyone gives even a cup of cold water to one of these little ones who is my disciple, truly I tell you, that person will certainly not lose their reward."

New King James Version

24 "A disciple is not above his teacher, nor a servant above his master. 25 It is enough for a disciple that he be like his teacher, and a servant like his master. If they have called the master of the house Beelzebub, how much more will they call those of his household! 26 Therefore do not fear them. For there is nothing covered that will not be revealed, and hidden that will not be known.

27 "Whatever I tell you in the dark, speak in the light; and what you hear in the ear, preach on the housetops. 28 And do not fear those who kill the body but cannot kill the soul. But rather fear Him who is able to destroy both soul and body in hell. 29 Are not two sparrows sold for a copper coin? And not one of them falls to the ground apart from your Father's will. 30 But the very hairs of your head are all numbered. 31 Do not fear therefore; you are of more value than many sparrows.

32 "Therefore whoever confesses Me before men, him I will also confess before My Father who is in heaven. 33 But whoever denies Me before men, him I will also deny before My Father who is in heaven.

34 "Do not think that I came to bring peace on earth. I did not come to bring peace but a sword. 35 For I have come to 'set a man against his father, a daughter against her mother, and a daughter-in-law against her mother-in-law'; 36 and 'a man's enemies will be those of his own household.' 37 He who loves father or mother more than Me is not worthy of Me. And he who loves son or daughter more than Me is not worthy of Me. 38 And he who does not take his cross and follow after Me is not worthy of Me. 39 He who finds his life will lose it, and he who loses his life for My sake will find it.

40 "He who receives you receives Me, and he who receives Me receives Him who sent Me. 41 He who receives a prophet in the name of a prophet shall receive a prophet's reward. And he who receives a righteous man in the name of a righteous man shall receive a righteous man's reward. 42 And whoever gives one of these little ones only a cup of cold water in the name of a disciple, assuredly, I say to you, he shall by no means lose his reward."

EXPLORATION

1. What is the disturbing "promise" that Jesus gives in verses 24–25?

2. Why does Jesus suggest it is foolish to be afraid of people?

3. What examples does Jesus use to convey the idea that God really is looking out for us?

4. What rewards does Christ promise to those who faithfully follow him?

5. What does Jesus say is the cost for following him? What does it mean to "take up your cross" and follow him?

6. Looking back over this section, do you find it more disturbing or more comforting? Why?

_____

_____

_____

_____

INSPIRATION

The story is told of a man on an African safari deep in the jungle. The guide before him had a machete and was whacking away the tall weeds and thick underbrush. The traveler, wearied and hot, asked in frustration, "Where are we? Do you know where you are taking me? Where is the path?!" The seasoned guide stopped and looked back at the man and replied, "I am the path."

We ask the same questions, don't we? We ask God, "Where are you taking me? Where is the path?" And he, like the guide, doesn't tell us. Oh, he may give us a hint or two, but that's all. If he did, would we understand? Would we comprehend our location? No, like the traveler, we are unacquainted with this jungle. So rather than give us an answer, Jesus gives us a far greater gift. He gives us himself.

Does he remove the jungle? No, the vegetation is still thick.

Does he purge the predators? No, danger still lurks. Jesus doesn't give hope by changing the jungle; he restores our hope by giving us himself. And he has promised to stay until the very end. *"I am with you always, to the very end of the age"* (Matthew 28:20).

We need that reminder. We all need that reminder. For all of us need hope.

Some of you don't need it right now. Your jungle has become a meadow and your journey a delight. If such is the case, congratulations. But remember—we do not know what tomorrow holds. We do not know where this road will lead. You may be one turn from a cemetery, from a hospital bed, from an empty house. You may be a bend in the road from a jungle. And though you don't need your hope restored today, you may tomorrow. And you need to know to whom to turn.

Or perhaps you do need hope today. You know you were not made for this place. You know you are not equipped. You want someone to lead you out. If so, call out for your Shepherd. He knows your voice. And he's just waiting for your request. (From *Traveling Light* by Max Lucado.)

REACTION

7. Does following Christ ever feel like this to you—like hacking your way through a wild jungle with no clear sense of direction? Why?

_____

_____

_____

_____

8. Given Jesus' stark and sobering in Matthew 10:24–42, what kind of reception should you expect as you live out your faith in the world, at work, in the neighborhood, at school?

_____

_____

_____

9. What are some specific ways a follower of Jesus can acknowledge him before other people?

_____

_____

10. What do you think Jesus means when he speaks of losing your life for his sake? It sounds radical and scary—but what does this look like in everyday terms?

11. What have been the highlights and lowlights in your time as a follower of Jesus?

12. What are your most consistent struggles in trying to walk with Christ on a daily basis?

LIFE LESSONS

We need to remember the first disciples were ordinary men called to an extraordinary mission. Before we turned them into stain-glassed saints in the windows of our cathedrals, Peter, John, and all the rest were just regular guys, trying to make a living and get along in life. They weren't seminary grads or spiritual giants. They didn't possess superhuman qualities. The most we can say about them is that their devotion to Jesus outweighed—by a hair—their fears and insecurities. As a result, God changed them and used them to accomplish some mind-boggling things. Why couldn't God—why *wouldn't* God—do the same thing in and through you and me?

DEVOTION

Lord, you haven't called me to a life of ease and comfort. You have called me to a life of trust and obedience. Help me to grow in you. Help me to daily know what it means to take up my cross and follow you. And help me resist the common but erroneous notion that following you will be anything but difficult.

JOURNALING

What are your biggest struggles just now? In light of what you've just studied, how might God be working in spite of your troubles?

FOR FURTHER READING

To complete the book of Matthew during this twelve-part study, read Matthew 10:1–42. For more Bible passages on what it means to follow Christ, read Psalm 15; Mark 8:34; Luke 14:25–35; and 2 Timothy 2:1–7.

LESSON SIX

HEAVEN'S GREAT INVITATION

*"Come to me, all you who are weary and
burdened, and I will give you rest."*
MATTHEW 11:28

REFLECTION

Invitations to join this club or that . . . requests for our presence at a party this weekend or a wedding next month . . . proposals for a deal here or a partnership there . . . life is filled with offers. What are some of the best invitations you've ever received? What have been the worst?

_____

_____

_____

_____

SITUATION

Since the time of Moses, Israel had been in possession of God's law, including the Lord's clear-cut commands and provisions for the Sabbath, the weekly day of rest and reflection. But over the centuries, the Jewish leaders had turned it all into a confusing and soul-destroying system. Then Jesus entered the scene and made a startling invitation.

OBSERVATION

Read Matthew 11:16–30 from the New International
Version or the New King James Version.

NEW INTERNATIONAL VERSION

¹⁶ "To what can I compare this generation? They are like children sitting in the marketplaces and calling out to others:

> ¹⁷ "'We played the pipe for you,
>   and you did not dance;
> we sang a dirge,
>   and you did not mourn.'

¹⁸ For John came neither eating nor drinking, and they say, 'He has a demon.' ¹⁹ The Son of Man came eating and drinking, and they say, 'Here is a glutton and a drunkard, a friend of tax collectors and sinners.' But wisdom is proved right by her deeds."

²⁰ Then Jesus began to denounce the towns in which most of his miracles had been performed, because they did not repent. ²¹ "Woe to you, Chorazin! Woe to you, Bethsaida! For if the miracles that were performed in you had been performed in Tyre and Sidon, they would have repented long ago in sackcloth and ashes. ²² But I tell you, it will be more bearable for Tyre and Sidon on the day of judgment than for you. ²³ And you, Capernaum, will you be lifted to the heavens? No, you will go down to Hades. For if the miracles that were performed in you had been performed in Sodom, it would have remained to this day. ²⁴ But I tell you that it will be more bearable for Sodom on the day of judgment than for you."

²⁵ At that time Jesus said, "I praise you, Father, Lord of heaven and earth, because you have hidden these things from the wise and learned, and revealed them to little children. ²⁶ Yes, Father, for this is what you were pleased to do.

²⁷ "All things have been committed to me by my Father. No one knows the Son except the Father, and no one knows the Father except the Son and those to whom the Son chooses to reveal him.

²⁸ "Come to me, all you who are weary and burdened, and I will give you rest. ²⁹ Take my yoke upon you and learn from me, for I am gentle and humble in heart, and you will find rest for your souls. ³⁰ For my yoke is easy and my burden is light."

New King James Version

¹⁶ "But to what shall I liken this generation? It is like children sitting in the marketplaces and calling to their companions, ¹⁷ and saying:

> 'We played the flute for you,
>   And you did not dance;
> We mourned to you,
>   And you did not lament.'

¹⁸ For John came neither eating nor drinking, and they say, 'He has a demon.' ¹⁹ The Son of Man came eating and drinking, and they say, 'Look, a glutton and a winebibber, a friend of tax collectors and sinners!' But wisdom is justified by her children."

²⁰ Then He began to rebuke the cities in which most of His mighty works had been done, because they did not repent: ²¹ "Woe to you, Chorazin! Woe to you, Bethsaida! For if the mighty works which were done in you had been done in Tyre and Sidon, they would have repented long ago in sackcloth and ashes. ²² But I say to you, it will be more tolerable for Tyre and Sidon in the day of judgment than for you. ²³ And you, Capernaum, who are exalted to heaven, will be brought down to Hades; for if the mighty works which were done in you had been done in Sodom, it would have remained until this day. ²⁴ But I say to you that it shall be more tolerable for the land of Sodom in the day of judgment than for you."

²⁵ At that time Jesus answered and said, "I thank You, Father, Lord of heaven and earth, that You have hidden these things from the wise and prudent and have revealed them to babes. ²⁶ Even so, Father, for so it seemed good in Your sight. ²⁷ All things have been delivered to Me by My Father, and no one knows the Son except the Father. Nor does anyone know the Father except the Son, and the one to whom the Son wills to reveal Him. ²⁸ Come to Me, all you who labor and are heavy laden, and I will give you rest. ²⁹ Take My yoke upon you and learn from Me, for I am gentle and lowly in heart, and you will find rest for your souls. ³⁰ For My yoke is easy and My burden is light."

EXPLORATION

1. What does Jesus reveal about human nature in verses 16–17?

2. How did Jesus say the people had responded to John the Baptist? How did he say the people had responded to his ministry?

3. Why did Jesus denounce so many of the cities in which he had ministered?

4. What do you make of Jesus' prayer in verses 25–26? What is he really saying in these verses?

5. To whom does Christ extend his gracious invitation?

6. What does this invitation tell you about the heart of God?

INSPIRATION

Invitations. Words embossed on a letter: "You are invited to a gala celebrating the grand opening of . . ." Requests received in the mail: "Mr. and Mrs. John Smith request your presence at the wedding of their daughter . . ." Surprises over the phone: "Hey, Joe. I've got an extra ticket to the game. Interested?"

To receive an invitation is to be honored—to be held in high esteem. For that reason all invitations deserve a kind and thoughtful response.

But the most incredible invitations are not found in envelopes or fortune cookies, they are found in the Bible. You can't read about God without finding him issuing invitations. He invited Eve to marry Adam, the animals to enter the ark, David to be king, Israel to leave bondage, Nehemiah to rebuild Jerusalem. God is an inviting God. He invited Mary to birth his son, the disciples to fish for men, the adulterous woman to start over, and Thomas to touch his wounds. God is the King who prepares the palace, sets the table, and invites his subjects to come in.

In fact, it seems his favorite word is *come*.

"*Come* now, let us settle the matter. . . . Though your sins are like scarlet, they shall be as white as snow" (Isaiah 1:18).

"*Come*, all you who are thirsty, come to the waters" (Isaiah 55:1).

"*Come* to me, all you who are weary and burdened, and I will give you rest" (Matthew 11:28).

"*Come* to the wedding banquet" (Matthew 22:4).

"*Come*, follow me . . . and I will send you out to fish for people" (Mark 1:17).

"Let anyone who is thirsty *come* to me and drink" (John 7:37).

God is a God who invites. God is a God who calls. God is a God who opens the door and waves his hand, pointing pilgrims to a full table.

His invitation is not just for a meal, however, it is for life. An invitation to come into his kingdom and take up residence in a tearless, graveless, painless world.

Who can come? Whoever wishes. The invitation is at once universal and personal. (From *And the Angels Were Silent* by Max Lucado.)

REACTION

7. What do you remember about the first time you ever comprehended and responded to Christ's invitation to come to him?

8. What is Jesus' "yoke"? What does he mean when he says it is "easy"? Easy compared to what?

9. In what ways do modern Christians (and churches) repeat the errors of the Pharisees and create a religious system that wears people out?

10. What sorts of daily burdens bring the most weariness to your soul?

11. When have you experienced genuine soul rest to the deepest degree? To what do you attribute this?

_____

_____

_____

_____

12. What counsel would you give to someone who said, "I'm at the end of my rope. I'm burned out. Please, help me. Tell me what to do"?

_____

_____

_____

_____

LIFE LESSONS

Christ looked into the leathery faces of farmers and weary faces of housewives and offered rest. The crowds came. They poured out of the cul-de-sacs and office complexes of their day. They brought him the burdens of their existence, and he gave them not religion, not doctrine, not systems, but rest. Today, Christ continues to look into the disillusioned eyes of the churchgoer, the cynical stare of a banker, and the hungry eyes of a bartender. And his paradoxical invitation still stands: "Take my yoke upon you and learn from me, for I am gentle and humble in heart, and you will find rest for your souls" (Matthew 11:29).

DEVOTION

Father, I want to trade my burdens—all my man-made rules and self-imposed religious obligations—for the true rest that you promised. Thank you for the constant invitation to come to you. Grant me the wisdom and courage to live as you intended so that I might attract others to you and not repel them.

JOURNALING

First Peter 5:7 states, "Cast all your anxiety on him because he cares for you." How can you give all your worries to God? If you did this, how much more "restful"—how much less anxious—would your soul be?

FOR FURTHER READING

To complete the book of Matthew during this twelve-part study, read Matthew 11:1–12:50. For more Bible passages on rest, read Exodus 23:12; Psalm 62; Isaiah 30:15; and Hebrews 4.

SPIRITUAL RECEPTIVITY

"It has been given to you to know the mysteries of the kingdom of heaven, but to them it has not been given. For whoever has, to him more will be given, and he will have abundance; but whoever does not have, even what he has will be taken away from him."

MATTHEW 13:11–12 NKJV

REFLECTION

The Bible is filled with agricultural imagery. Ours is not the agrarian society it used to be, but spending on lawn-and-garden supplies has nevertheless skyrocketed over the years. If you have much experience growing in flowers, fruit, or vegetables, what have you found to be the secret to success in the yard or garden?

SITUATION

The kingdom of heaven was a source of great hope for the Jewish people. And yet, this much-discussed subject was also a matter of major misunderstanding. Jesus addressed the problem by telling short stories called *parables*. Within these short stories, he employed common, everyday objects and activities to illustrate various truths about God's kingdom.

OBSERVATION

Read Matthew 13:3–23 from the New International Version or the New King James Version.

New International Version

³ Then he told them many things in parables, saying: "A farmer went out to sow his seed. ⁴ As he was scattering the seed, some fell along the path, and the birds came and ate it up. ⁵ Some fell on rocky places, where it did not have much soil. It sprang up quickly, because the soil was shallow. ⁶ But when the sun came up, the plants were scorched, and they withered because they had no root. ⁷ Other seed fell among thorns,

which grew up and choked the plants. [8] Still other seed fell on good soil, where it produced a crop—a hundred, sixty or thirty times what was sown. [9] Whoever has ears, let them hear."

[10] The disciples came to him and asked, "Why do you speak to the people in parables?"

[11] He replied, "Because the knowledge of the secrets of the kingdom of heaven has been given to you, but not to them. [12] Whoever has will be given more, and they will have an abundance. Whoever does not have, even what they have will be taken from them. [13] This is why I speak to them in parables:

"Though seeing, they do not see;
  though hearing, they do not hear or understand.

[14] In them is fulfilled the prophecy of Isaiah:

"'You will be ever hearing but never understanding;
  you will be ever seeing but never perceiving.
[15] For this people's heart has become calloused;
  they hardly hear with their ears,
  and they have closed their eyes.
Otherwise they might see with their eyes,
  hear with their ears,
  understand with their hearts
and turn, and I would heal them.'

[16] But blessed are your eyes because they see, and your ears because they hear. [17] For truly I tell you, many prophets and righteous people longed to see what you see but did not see it, and to hear what you hear but did not hear it.

[18] "Listen then to what the parable of the sower means: [19] When anyone hears the message about the kingdom and does not understand it, the evil one comes and snatches away what was sown in their heart. This is the seed sown along the path. [20] The seed falling on rocky ground refers

to someone who hears the word and at once receives it with joy. [21] But since they have no root, they last only a short time. When trouble or persecution comes because of the word, they quickly fall away. [22] The seed falling among the thorns refers to someone who hears the word, but the worries of this life and the deceitfulness of wealth choke the word, making it unfruitful. [23] But the seed falling on good soil refers to someone who hears the word and understands it. This is the one who produces a crop, yielding a hundred, sixty or thirty times what was sown."

NEW KING JAMES VERSION

[3] Then He spoke many things to them in parables, saying: "Behold, a sower went out to sow. [4] And as he sowed, some seed fell by the wayside; and the birds came and devoured them. [5] Some fell on stony places, where they did not have much earth; and they immediately sprang up because they had no depth of earth. [6] But when the sun was up they were scorched, and because they had no root they withered away. [7] And some fell among thorns, and the thorns sprang up and choked them. [8] But others fell on good ground and yielded a crop: some a hundredfold, some sixty, some thirty. [9] He who has ears to hear, let him hear!"

[10] And the disciples came and said to Him, "Why do You speak to them in parables?"

[11] He answered and said to them, "Because it has been given to you to know the mysteries of the kingdom of heaven, but to them it has not been given. [12] For whoever has, to him more will be given, and he will have abundance; but whoever does not have, even what he has will be taken away from him. [13] Therefore I speak to them in parables, because seeing they do not see, and hearing they do not hear, nor do they understand. [14] And in them the prophecy of Isaiah is fulfilled, which says:

'Hearing you will hear and shall not understand,
And seeing you will see and not perceive;
[15] For the hearts of this people have grown dull.
Their ears are hard of hearing,

> And their eyes they have closed,
> Lest they should see with their eyes and hear with their ears,
> Lest they should understand with their hearts and turn,
> So that I should heal them.'

[16] But blessed are your eyes for they see, and your ears for they hear; [17] for assuredly, I say to you that many prophets and righteous men desired to see what you see, and did not see it, and to hear what you hear, and did not hear it.

[18] "Therefore hear the parable of the sower: [19] When anyone hears the word of the kingdom, and does not understand it, then the wicked one comes and snatches away what was sown in his heart. This is he who received seed by the wayside. [20] But he who received the seed on stony places, this is he who hears the word and immediately receives it with joy; [21] yet he has no root in himself, but endures only for a while. For when tribulation or persecution arises because of the word, immediately he stumbles. [22] Now he who received seed among the thorns is he who hears the word, and the cares of this world and the deceitfulness of riches choke the word, and he becomes unfruitful. [23] But he who received seed on the good ground is he who hears the word and understands it, who indeed bears fruit and produces: some a hundredfold, some sixty, some thirty."

EXPLORATION

1. What happened in the story of the seed-sowing farmer?

2. What factors determined whether the seed bore fruit?

3. Why did Jesus say he relied so heavily on parables in his teaching?

_____

_____

_____

4. Why did Jesus say the disciples were blessed? What did they have that the masses did not?

_____

_____

_____

5. How did Jesus explain the underlying meaning of the parable of the four soils?

_____

_____

_____

6. According to Jesus, why is it not enough for a person to be exposed to the Word of God?

_____

_____

INSPIRATION

To the Hebrew mind, the heart is a freeway cloverleaf where all emotions and prejudices and wisdom converge. It is a switch house that receives freight cars loaded with moods, ideas, emotions, and convictions and puts them on the right track.

And just as a low-grade oil or alloyed gasoline would cause you to question the performance of a refinery, evil acts and impure thoughts cause us to question the condition of our hearts. . . . The heart is the center of the spiritual life. If the fruit of a tree is bad, you don't try to fix the fruit; you treat the roots. And if a person's actions are evil, it's not enough to change habits; you have to go deeper. You have to go to the heart of the problem, which is the problem of the heart.

That is why the state of the heart is so critical. What's the state of yours?

When someone barks at you, do you bark back or bite your tongue? That depends on the state of your heart.

When your schedule is too tight or your to-do list too long, do you lose your cool or keep it? That depends on the state of your heart.

When you are offered a morsel of gossip marinated in slander, do you turn it down or pass it on? That depends on the state of your heart.

Do you see the bag lady on the street as a burden on society or as an opportunity for God? That, too, depends on the state of your heart.

The state of your heart dictates whether you harbor a grudge or give grace, seek self-pity or seek Christ, drink human misery or taste God's mercy. No wonder, then, the wise man begs, "Above all else, guard your heart" (Proverbs 4:23).

David's prayer should be ours: "Create in me a pure heart, O God" (Psalm 51:10).

And Jesus' statement rings true: "Blessed are the pure in heart, for they shall see God." (From *The Applause of Heaven* by Max Lucado.)

REACTION

7. A thousand people can hear the same sermon, but only five in the crowd will truly be impacted and changed. What do you think makes the difference?

_____

_____

8. How do each of the four soils differ from one another?

_____

_____

9. What is necessary for people to change if they realize the soil of their heart is not conducive to growth or that their life is barren of fruit?

_____

_____

10. What does fruitfulness and abundance look like in a life that is yielded to God?

_____

_____

11. Compare your life to the soils described by Jesus. Which soil is closest to you?

_____

_____

12. How do the worries of this life and the deceitfulness of wealth choke the Word of God? How does a citizen of the kingdom of heaven guard against these things?

_____

_____

LIFE LESSONS

The kingdom of God has both a present and a future aspect. During his first coming, Jesus fulfilled the role of a suffering servant. Through his death on the cross, he defeated the kingdom of darkness and made it possible for sinners to be forgiven and brought into his spiritual kingdom. He currently rules quietly in the hearts of those who are responsive to him—those who collectively make up his church. But at his second coming, Christ will rule all things. His kingdom then will be visible and universal, and it will never end. By letting his Word take root in our hearts, we bear fruit for God. Through a kind of spiritual cultivation we are to watch over our souls, keeping them from becoming hard or hostile to the truth and rooting out any weeds of worldliness that can choke the fruit of righteousness.

DEVOTION

Father, protect me from the evil one. Keep me from spiritual indifference and shallowness. Make me aware and intolerant of worldly attitudes. Give me an ever-deepening desire to receive your Word with great eagerness. May it take root deeply in my soul so that I bear lasting fruit for your glory.

JOURNALING

What are the worries of this world that threaten to make you unfruitful in your faith?

FOR FURTHER READING

To complete the book of Matthew during this twelve-part study, read Matthew 13:1–52. For more Bible passages on fruitfulness, read Hosea 10:11–12; Luke 3:8–9; 13:6–9; John 15; Galatians 5:22–23; and Colossians 1:10.

LESSON EIGHT

BREAD OF LIFE

They all ate and were satisfied, and the disciples picked
up twelve basketfuls of broken pieces that were left over.
MATTHEW 14:20

REFLECTION

Food is such a dominant part of daily life. When it's missing, we notice! Think about a time when you've gone without food, either by choice or by necessity. What was the experience like of being hungry and then being able to eat again?

_____

_____

_____

SITUATION

The day starts with some tragic news. John the Baptist has just been executed by Herod Antipas, the reigning monarch. When Jesus hears the news, he retreats to a solitary place to be alone. Against this backdrop, Matthew describes how Jesus then revealed the depth of his power and compassion. The Carpenter King feeds a crowd of 5,000 men (plus women and children) with five loaves and two fish. In the process, he teaches his disciples an important lesson on faith and caring for those in need.

OBSERVATION

Read Matthew 14:6–21 from the New International
Version or the New King James Version.

NEW INTERNATIONAL VERSION
⁶ On Herod's birthday the daughter of Herodias danced for the guests and pleased Herod so much ⁷ that he promised with an oath to give her whatever she asked. ⁸ Prompted by her mother, she said, "Give me here on a platter the head of John the Baptist." ⁹ The king was distressed, but because of his oaths and his dinner guests, he ordered that her re-

quest be granted [10] and had John beheaded in the prison. [11] His head was brought in on a platter and given to the girl, who carried it to her mother. [12] John's disciples came and took his body and buried it. Then they went and told Jesus.

[13] When Jesus heard what had happened, he withdrew by boat privately to a solitary place. Hearing of this, the crowds followed him on foot from the towns. [14] When Jesus landed and saw a large crowd, he had compassion on them and healed their sick.

[15] As evening approached, the disciples came to him and said, "This is a remote place, and it's already getting late. Send the crowds away, so they can go to the villages and buy themselves some food."

[16] Jesus replied, "They do not need to go away. You give them something to eat."

[17] "We have here only five loaves of bread and two fish," they answered.

[18] "Bring them here to me," he said. [19] And he directed the people to sit down on the grass. Taking the five loaves and the two fish and looking up to heaven, he gave thanks and broke the loaves. Then he gave them to the disciples, and the disciples gave them to the people. [20] They all ate and were satisfied, and the disciples picked up twelve basketfuls of broken pieces that were left over. [21] The number of those who ate was about five thousand men, besides women and children.

NEW KING JAMES VERSION

[6] But when Herod's birthday was celebrated, the daughter of Herodias danced before them and pleased Herod. [7] Therefore he promised with an oath to give her whatever she might ask.

[8] So she, having been prompted by her mother, said, "Give me John the Baptist's head here on a platter."

[9] And the king was sorry; nevertheless, because of the oaths and because of those who sat with him, he commanded it to be given to her. [10] So he sent and had John beheaded in prison. [11] And his head was brought on a platter and given to the girl, and she brought it to her mother. [12] Then his disciples came and took away the body and buried it, and went and told Jesus.

¹³ When Jesus heard it, He departed from there by boat to a deserted place by Himself. But when the multitudes heard it, they followed Him on foot from the cities. ¹⁴ And when Jesus went out He saw a great multitude; and He was moved with compassion for them, and healed their sick. ¹⁵ When it was evening, His disciples came to Him, saying, "This is a deserted place, and the hour is already late. Send the multitudes away, that they may go into the villages and buy themselves food."

¹⁶ But Jesus said to them, "They do not need to go away. You give them something to eat."

¹⁷ And they said to Him, "We have here only five loaves and two fish."

¹⁸ He said, "Bring them here to Me." ¹⁹ Then He commanded the multitudes to sit down on the grass. And He took the five loaves and the two fish, and looking up to heaven, He blessed and broke and gave the loaves to the disciples; and the disciples gave to the multitudes. ²⁰ So they all ate and were filled, and they took up twelve baskets full of the fragments that remained. ²¹ Now those who had eaten were about five thousand men, besides women and children.

EXPLORATION

1. Herod Antipas had ordered John the Baptist to be imprisoned because he had said it was not lawful for him to be married to his brother's wife (see Matthew 14:1–5). What events led to Herod reluctantly agreeing to have John executed?

_____

_____

_____

_____

2. Why did Herod feel he had to honor his daughter's request?

_____

_____

_____

3. What was Jesus' response to the report of John's death?

4. How did the masses react when they learned Jesus had left by boat?

5. What was the disciples' attitude and recommendation when the day had ended and the crowds were still there?

6. How did Jesus ultimately deal with all those hungry people who had followed him to a remote location?

INSPIRATION

The feeding of the five thousand . . . answers the question, *What does God do when his children are weak?* If God ever needed an excuse to give up on people, he has one here. Surely God is going to banish these followers until they learn to believe.

Is that what he does? You decide. "Jesus then took the loaves, gave thanks, and distributed to those who were seated as much as they wanted. He did the same with the fish" (John 6:11).

When the disciples didn't pray, Jesus prayed. When the disciples didn't see God, Jesus sought God. When the disciples were weak, Jesus was strong. When the disciples had no faith, Jesus had faith. He thanked God.

For what? The crowds? The pandemonium? The weariness? The faithless disciples? No, he thanked God for the basket of bread. He ignored the clouds and found the ray and thanked God for it.

Look what he does next. "Taking the five loaves and the two fish and looking up to heaven, he gave thanks and broke the loaves. Then he gave them to the disciples, and the disciples gave them to the people" (Matthew 14:19).

Rather than punish the disciples, he employs them. There they go, passing out the bread they didn't request, enjoying the answer to the prayer they didn't even pray. If Jesus would have acted according to the faith of his disciples, the multitudes would have gone unfed. But he didn't, and he doesn't. God is true to us even when we forget him.

God's blessings are dispensed according to the riches of his grace, not according to the depth of our faith. "If we are faithless, he remains faithful, for he cannot disown himself" (2 Timothy 2:13).

Why is that important to know? So you won't get cynical. Look around you. Aren't there more mouths than bread? Aren't there more wounds than physicians? Aren't there more who need the truth than those who tell it? Aren't there more churches asleep than churches afire?

So what do we do? Throw up our hands and walk away? Tell the world we can't help them? That's what the disciples wanted to do. Should we just give up . . . ? No, we don't give up. We look up. We trust. We believe. And our optimism is not hollow. Christ has proven worthy. He has shown that he never fails, though there is nothing but failure in us.

God is faithful even when his children are not. (From *A Gentle Thunder* by Max Lucado.)

REACTION

7. John the Baptist and Jesus were both cousins and colleagues. What emotions do you think Jesus must have been feeling when he heard about John's brutal execution?

_____

_____

_____

_____

_____

8. How does Jesus' response in this situation epitomize the concept of compassionate and selfless servanthood?

_____

_____

_____

_____

9. How and where do you find the capacity to give, serve, and be centered on others when you are battling your own trials and tragedies?

_____

_____

_____

_____

10. Summarize the overall reaction of the disciples to this series of incidents. In what ways can you relate to their attitudes and actions?

_____

11. There is a tension in this passage between Christ's desire to commune with his Father and the needs of the people around him. How do we balance these competing needs—our own souls for rest and replenishment and the endless demands (many legitimate) of others?

_____

_____

_____

_____

_____

12. Matthew notes in verse 19 that Jesus directed the people to sit on the grass. Mark 6:39 adds the little detail that it was "green" grass. What does this often overlooked fact remind us about the one known as the Good Shepherd (see Psalm 23)?

_____

_____

_____

_____

LIFE LESSONS

Life is messy and hard. People are needy and demanding. We are called to lives of sacrifice and service. How do we pull it off? Like the disciples of old, we follow the One with all the power and compassion. We look to him. We listen to him. We do whatever he tells us. Ultimately, we trust him to work through us. Such a life is scary and uncertain. We will be tested and pulled. But in the end, our faith will grow and the needs of others will be met. The one fact we must cling to is that Jesus is the bread of God who comes down from heaven and gives life to the world (see John 6:33).

DEVOTION

Lord Jesus, you are the Bread of Life who gives life to the world. Give me the good sense to come to you daily and draw my strength from you. You are the Good Shepherd. Grant me the courage to follow your example so that I might serve others and lead them to you.

JOURNALING

Someone wisely said, "You cannot impart what you do not possess." What do you need to do to become a more effective servant to others and a more compelling witness to God's goodness?

FOR FURTHER READING

To complete the book of Matthew during this twelve-part study, read Matthew 13:53–17:27. For more Bible passages on spiritual food, read Exodus 16:1–35; Isaiah 25; John 4:31–34; 6:27; and Hebrews 5:12–14.

HUMILITY

"Assuredly, I say to you, unless you are converted and become as little children, you will by no means enter the kingdom of heaven. Therefore whoever humbles himself as this little child is the greatest in the kingdom of heaven."

MATTHEW 18:3–4 NKJV

REFLECTION

Mother Teresa gained worldwide recognition during her lifetime for her tireless work among the poorest of the poor in the streets of Calcutta, India. What admirable qualities did she possess? Why do you think her story stands out in people's minds even today?

_____

_____

_____

SITUATION

During the time of Christ, Israel was under the authority of the Roman Empire. Honor, power, pride, prestige, acclaim were all the dominant values of Rome. Not surprisingly, Jesus advocated and modeled a different value system for his followers. The ways of the world are not the ways of the kingdom of Christ.

OBSERVATION

Read Matthew 18:1–14 from the New International Version or the New King James Version.

NEW INTERNATIONAL VERSION

[1] At that time the disciples came to Jesus and asked, "Who, then, is the greatest in the kingdom of heaven?"

[2] He called a little child to him, and placed the child among them. [3] And he said: "Truly I tell you, unless you change and become like little children, you will never enter the kingdom of heaven. [4] Therefore, whoever takes the lowly position of this child is the greatest in the

kingdom of heaven. [5] And whoever welcomes one such child in my name welcomes me.

[6] "If anyone causes one of these little ones—those who believe in me—to stumble, it would be better for them to have a large millstone hung around their neck and to be drowned in the depths of the sea. [7] Woe to the world because of the things that cause people to stumble! Such things must come, but woe to the person through whom they come! [8] If your hand or your foot causes you to stumble, cut it off and throw it away. It is better for you to enter life maimed or crippled than to have two hands or two feet and be thrown into eternal fire. [9] And if your eye causes you to stumble, gouge it out and throw it away. It is better for you to enter life with one eye than to have two eyes and be thrown into the fire of hell.

[10] "See that you do not despise one of these little ones. For I tell you that their angels in heaven always see the face of my Father in heaven. [[11]]

[12] "What do you think? If a man owns a hundred sheep, and one of them wanders away, will he not leave the ninety-nine on the hills and go to look for the one that wandered off? [13] And if he finds it, truly I tell you, he is happier about that one sheep than about the ninety-nine that did not wander off. [14] In the same way your Father in heaven is not willing that any of these little ones should perish.

NEW KING JAMES VERSION
[1] At that time the disciples came to Jesus, saying, "Who then is greatest in the kingdom of heaven?"

[2] Then Jesus called a little child to Him, set him in the midst of them, [3] and said, "Assuredly, I say to you, unless you are converted and become as little children, you will by no means enter the kingdom of heaven. [4] Therefore whoever humbles himself as this little child is the greatest in the kingdom of heaven. [5] Whoever receives one little child like this in My name receives Me.

[6] "Whoever causes one of these little ones who believe in Me to sin, it would be better for him if a millstone were hung around his neck, and he were drowned in the depth of the sea. [7] Woe to the world because

of offenses! For offenses must come, but woe to that man by whom the offense comes!

⁸ "If your hand or foot causes you to sin, cut it off and cast it from you. It is better for you to enter into life lame or maimed, rather than having two hands or two feet, to be cast into the everlasting fire. ⁹ And if your eye causes you to sin, pluck it out and cast it from you. It is better for you to enter into life with one eye, rather than having two eyes, to be cast into hell fire.

¹⁰ "Take heed that you do not despise one of these little ones, for I say to you that in heaven their angels always see the face of My Father who is in heaven. ¹¹ For the Son of Man has come to save that which was lost.

¹² "What do you think? If a man has a hundred sheep, and one of them goes astray, does he not leave the ninety-nine and go to the mountains to seek the one that is straying? ¹³ And if he should find it, assuredly, I say to you, he rejoices more over that sheep than over the ninety-nine that did not go astray. ¹⁴ Even so it is not the will of your Father who is in heaven that one of these little ones should perish.

EXPLORATION

1. What topic were the disciples discussing that they wanted an answer from Jesus?

2. How did Jesus settle their dispute? What quality did he call them to demonstrate?

3. How did Jesus inject an eternal perspective into this conversation?

4. According to Jesus, who is great in God's eyes?

5. How did Jesus illustrate the importance of "lowly" and "forgotten" people like children?

6. What does the parable of the lost sheep reveal about how God cares for everyone?

INSPIRATION

Deflating inflated egos is so important to God that he offers to help.

He helped me. I recently spent an autumn week on a book tour. We saw long lines and crowded stores. One person after another complimented me. For three days I bathed in the river of praise. I began to believe the accolades. *All these people can't be wrong. I must be God's gift to readers.*

My chest puffed so much I could hardly see where to autograph the books. Why, had I been born 2,000 years earlier, we might read the gospels of Matthew, Max, Luke, and John. About the time I wondered if the Bible needed another epistle, God shot an arrow of humility in my direction.

We were running late for an evening book signing—late because the afternoon book signing had seen such long lines. We expected the same at the next store. Concerned, we phoned ahead. "We are running behind. Tell all the people we'll arrive soon."

"No need to hurry," the store manager assured.

"What about the people?" we asked.

"Neither one seems to be in a hurry."

Neither one?

By the time we reached the store, thankfully, the crowd of two people had tripled to six. We had scheduled two hours for the signing; I needed ten minutes.

Self-conscious about sitting alone at the table, I peppered the last person with questions. We talked about her parents, school, Social Security number, favorite birthday party. Against my pleadings, she had to go. So I sat alone at the table. Big stack of Lucado books, no one in line.

I asked the store manager, "Did you advertise?" "We did. More than usual." She walked off.

The next time she passed I asked, "Had other signings?" "Yes, usually we have a great response," and kept going.

I signed all the books at my table. I signed all the Lucado books on the shelves. I signed Tom Clancy and John Grisham books. Finally a customer came to the table. "You write books?" he asked, picking up the new one.

"I do. Want me to sign it?"

"No thanks," he answered and left.

God hit his target. Lest I forget, my daily reading the next morning had this passage: "Do not be wise in your own eyes" (Proverbs 3:7 NKJV).

When you're full of yourself, God can't fill you. (From *Cure for the Common Life* by Max Lucado.)

REACTION

7. Why do you think we get so full of ourselves so often?

8. How would you describe humility? Give some examples.

9. Our society is a bit different from the ancient Roman Empire. What are the dominant values that our neighbors and colleagues live by?

10. What are the risks of living humbly and showing extraordinary kindness to the "least of these"?

11. In *The Weight of Glory*, C. S. Lewis observed, "There are no ordinary people. You have never talked to a mere mortal. Nations, cultures, arts, civilizations—these are mortal, and their life is to ours as the life of a gnat. But it is immortals whom we joke with, work with, marry, snub, and exploit—immortal horrors or everlasting splendors." Why is it difficult to remember this and treat others—*all* others—with dignity and respect?

_____

_____

_____

_____

_____

12. What are the dangers of pride (see Proverbs 16:18)?

_____

_____

_____

LIFE LESSONS

We will either take our cues from the world or the Word. There are no other options. We can buy into the dominant temporal value system that says: *Be cutthroat. Compete. See all others as rivals. Promote yourself (by tearing others down). Pursue the acclaim of others.* Or we can embrace the rare and precious eternal value system that says: *Be Christ-like. Submit. See others as those whom you can serve. Live to promote Christ. Pursue the commendation of God.* The first way is the way of pride. The second way is the way of humility. The first way ends ironically in destruction. The second way culminates in exaltation.

DEVOTION

Lord, give me a discerning spirit and the transformed mindset necessary to see that things are not what they appear. Help me to say no to the constant temptation to promote myself. Remind me constantly that my calling is to promote you and that I do this by serving others using the gifts and opportunities you give.

JOURNALING

Who are some people God is nudging you to serve? What are some concrete ways that you can serve those individuals?

FOR FURTHER READING

To complete the book of Matthew during this twelve-part study, read Matthew 18:1–35. For more Bible passages on humility, read Psalm 18:27; Proverbs 11:2; 29:23; James 4:10; and 1 Peter 3:8.

LESSON TEN

MISSING THE MESSIAH

But when the chief priests and the teachers of
the law saw the wonderful things he did and the
children shouting in the temple courts, "Hosanna
to the Son of David," they were indignant.
MATTHEW 21:15

REFLECTION

Disappointment always stems from unmet expectations. Our level of disappointment in any situation is directly tied to the difference between what we hoped for and what actually happened. What are some of your biggest disappointments or letdowns in life?

_____

_____

_____

SITUATION

As Jesus' time on earth drew to a close, he entered Jerusalem as a king . . . but not the exalted monarch whom many would have preferred. He rode a humble donkey, not the white horse of a conqueror. Dismounting, he promptly caused a scene at the temple and incurred the wrath of Israel's religious leaders. These head-scratching events, coupled with Jesus' other odd sayings and unusual views, caused many to doubt his messianic claims.

OBSERVATION

Read Matthew 21:1–17 from the New International
Version or the New King James Version.

NEW INTERNATIONAL VERSION

[1] As they approached Jerusalem and came to Bethphage on the Mount of Olives, Jesus sent two disciples, [2] saying to them, "Go to the village ahead of you, and at once you will find a donkey tied there, with her colt

by her. Untie them and bring them to me. ³ If anyone says anything to you, say that the Lord needs them, and he will send them right away."

⁴ This took place to fulfill what was spoken through the prophet:

⁵ "Say to Daughter Zion,
　'See, your king comes to you,
　gentle and riding on a donkey,
　　and on a colt, the foal of a donkey.'"

⁶ The disciples went and did as Jesus had instructed them. ⁷ They brought the donkey and the colt and placed their cloaks on them for Jesus to sit on. ⁸ A very large crowd spread their cloaks on the road, while others cut branches from the trees and spread them on the road. ⁹ The crowds that went ahead of him and those that followed shouted,

"Hosanna to the Son of David!"
"Blessed is he who comes in the name of the Lord!"
"Hosanna in the highest heaven!"

¹⁰ When Jesus entered Jerusalem, the whole city was stirred and asked, "Who is this?"

¹¹ The crowds answered, "This is Jesus, the prophet from Nazareth in Galilee."

¹² Jesus entered the temple courts and drove out all who were buying and selling there. He overturned the tables of the money changers and the benches of those selling doves. ¹³ "It is written," he said to them, "'My house will be called a house of prayer,' but you are making it 'a den of robbers.'"

¹⁴ The blind and the lame came to him at the temple, and he healed them. ¹⁵ But when the chief priests and the teachers of the law saw the wonderful things he did and the children shouting in the temple courts, "Hosanna to the Son of David," they were indignant.

¹⁶ "Do you hear what these children are saying?" they asked him.

"Yes," replied Jesus, "have you never read,

"'From the lips of children and infants
      you, Lord, have called forth your praise'?"

[17] And he left them and went out of the city to Bethany, where he spent the night.

New King James Version

[1] Now when they drew near Jerusalem, and came to Bethphage, at the Mount of Olives, then Jesus sent two disciples, [2] saying to them, "Go into the village opposite you, and immediately you will find a donkey tied, and a colt with her. Loose them and bring them to Me. [3] And if anyone says anything to you, you shall say, 'The Lord has need of them,' and immediately he will send them."

[4] All this was done that it might be fulfilled which was spoken by the prophet, saying:

[5] "Tell the daughter of Zion,
   'Behold, your King is coming to you,
   Lowly, and sitting on a donkey,
   A colt, the foal of a donkey.'"

[6] So the disciples went and did as Jesus commanded them. [7] They brought the donkey and the colt, laid their clothes on them, and set Him on them. [8] And a very great multitude spread their clothes on the road; others cut down branches from the trees and spread them on the road. [9] Then the multitudes who went before and those who followed cried out, saying:

"Hosanna to the Son of David!
   'Blessed is He who comes in the name of the Lord!'
   Hosanna in the highest!"

¹⁰ And when He had come into Jerusalem, all the city was moved, saying, "Who is this?"

¹¹ So the multitudes said, "This is Jesus, the prophet from Nazareth of Galilee."

¹² Then Jesus went into the temple of God and drove out all those who bought and sold in the temple, and overturned the tables of the money changers and the seats of those who sold doves. ¹³ And He said to them, "It is written, 'My house shall be called a house of prayer,' but you have made it a 'den of thieves.'"

¹⁴ Then the blind and the lame came to Him in the temple, and He healed them. ¹⁵ But when the chief priests and scribes saw the wonderful things that He did, and the children crying out in the temple and saying, "Hosanna to the Son of David!" they were indignant ¹⁶ and said to Him, "Do You hear what these are saying?"

And Jesus said to them, "Yes. Have you never read,

> 'Out of the mouth of babes and nursing infants
> You have perfected praise'?"

¹⁷ Then He left them and went out of the city to Bethany, and He lodged there.

EXPLORATION

1. Do Jesus' instructions at the beginning of this passage strike you as a little odd? Put yourself in the sandals of one of those disciples. What are you feeling and thinking?

_____

_____

_____

_____

2. Prophecies in Isaiah 62:11 and Zechariah 9:9 both related how the Messiah would enter into Jerusalem riding on a donkey. Why didn't this fact alone convince all the masses who witnessed his entrance that Jesus was the Christ?

3. How did the multitudes respond when asked who Jesus was?

4. Why did Jesus get so angry when he entered the temple area?

5. What were the children doing during this temple-cleansing episode?

6. As all these odd, apparently conflicting events were going on, what do you think the followers of Jesus were doing—those who had spent the previous three years traveling with him, living with him, listening to him, and learning from him?

INSPIRATION

Some of us have tried to have a daily quiet time and have not been successful. Others of us have a hard time concentrating. And all of us are busy. So rather than spend time with God, listening for his voice, we'll let others spend time with him and then benefit from their experience. Let them tell us what God is saying. After all, isn't that why we pay preachers? Isn't that why we read Christian books? *These folks are good at daily devotions. I'll just learn from them.*

If that is your approach, if your spiritual experiences are secondhand and not firsthand, I'd like to challenge you with this thought: *Do you do that with other parts of your life?* I don't think so.

You don't do that with vacations. You don't say, "Vacations are such a hassle, packing bags and traveling. I'm going to send someone on vacation for me. When he returns, I'll hear all about it and be spared all the inconvenience." Would you do that? No! You want the experience firsthand. . . . Certain things no one can do for you.

You don't do that with romance. You don't say, "I'm in love with that wonderful person, but romance is such a hassle. I'm going to hire a surrogate lover to enjoy the romance in my place. I'll hear all about it and be spared the inconvenience." Who would do that? Perish the thought. You want the romance firsthand. . . . Certain things no one can do for you.

You don't let someone eat on your behalf, do you? You don't say, "Chewing is such a bother. My jaws grow so tired, and the variety of tastes is so overwhelming. I'm going to hire someone to chew my food, and I'll just swallow whatever he gives me." Would you do that? Yuck! Of course not! Certain things no one can do for you.

And one of those is spending time with God.

Listening to God is a firsthand experience. When he asks for your attention, God doesn't want you to send a substitute; he wants you. He invites *you* to vacation in his splendor. He invites *you* to feel the touch of his hand. He invites *you* to feast at his table. He wants to spend time with *you*. And with a little training, your time with God can be the highlight of your day. (From *Just Like Jesus* by Max Lucado.)

REACTION

7. Do most of your ideas about Christ come from what others have said about him or from your own personal interactions with him? Explain.

_____

_____

_____

_____

8. How can a secondhand faith lead to disappointment with Christ?

_____

_____

_____

_____

9. It is one thing to get excited about Jesus in a parade-like, rah-rah atmosphere. It is another matter altogether to be devoted to him and follow him daily. What factors keep you from a more personal relationship with Jesus?

_____

_____

_____

_____

10. One of the teachings of the New Testament is that Christians are God's temple (see 1 Corinthians 3:16–17; 6:19; 2 Corinthians 6:16). Given that fact, what kind of cleansing might Jesus like to do in your own soul?

_____

_____

_____

11. Picture a bunch of kids shouting in the reverent temple courts. What does this scenario teach us about worship, about celebration, and about excitement over the person of Christ?

_____

_____

_____

12. How can time with the Lord, which leads to deeper intimacy with him, minimize our feelings of disappointment with God?

_____

_____

_____

LIFE LESSONS

God will often surprise us or disappoint us because our expectations of him do not correspond with his will or with ultimate reality. We may have strong ideas (and wrong ideas) about how life should unfold, but then we crash head-on into God's purposes, and confusion sets in. The solution to this common dilemma is to surrender our opinions and hopes about *what should be* to *what actually is* in God's perfect plan. When we spend time getting to know the Lord firsthand, and then approach the situations of life with an open mind and a yielded spirit, we are able to avoid needless disappointment. Remember that God isn't whatever we want him to be. He is who he is. And he will do what he will do.

DEVOTION

Lord, so many people stood near you and watched you during your time on this earth, and yet they missed you! They allowed false expectations and the reports of others to keep them from a personal encounter with you. Don't let me make this same mistake. Stir my longing for you so I will pursue you with passion and come to know you as you truly are.

JOURNALING

What are some of your biggest disappointments in life? How have you sought to overcome those disappointments?

_____

_____

_____

_____

_____

_____

_____

_____

_____

_____

_____

_____

_____

FOR FURTHER READING

To complete the book of Matthew during this twelve-part study, read Matthew 19:1–23:39. For more Bible passages on knowing Christ as Messiah, read Matthew 12:22–23; and John 1:44–46; 4:29; 6:42.

LESSON ELEVEN

THE LAST DAYS

*Therefore you also be ready, for the Son of Man
is coming at an hour you do not expect.*
MATTHEW 24:44 NKJV

REFLECTION

Few subjects are as hotly debated among Christians as the subject of the "end times." Believers argue such questions as, *When will Christ return? What will be the sequence of events? What is Armageddon?* What is your current understanding of the last days?

SITUATION

During the final week before Jesus' crucifixion, he gathered his disciples and talked frankly to them about his second coming. Speaking from the Mount of Olives—where the prophet Zechariah had revealed the Messiah would stand when he comes again to establish his kingdom—he urged his followers to be ready for his return and to be faithful to the end.

OBSERVATION

Read Matthew 24:32–51 from the New International Version or the New King James Version.

NEW INTERNATIONAL VERSION

[32] "Now learn this lesson from the fig tree: As soon as its twigs get tender and its leaves come out, you know that summer is near. [33] Even so, when you see all these things, you know that it is near, right at the door. [34] Truly I tell you, this generation will certainly not pass away until all these things have happened. [35] Heaven and earth will pass away, but my words will never pass away.

³⁶ "But about that day or hour no one knows, not even the angels in heaven, nor the Son, but only the Father. ³⁷ As it was in the days of Noah, so it will be at the coming of the Son of Man. ³⁸ For in the days before the flood, people were eating and drinking, marrying and giving in marriage, up to the day Noah entered the ark; ³⁹ and they knew nothing about what would happen until the flood came and took them all away. That is how it will be at the coming of the Son of Man. ⁴⁰ Two men will be in the field; one will be taken and the other left. ⁴¹ Two women will be grinding with a hand mill; one will be taken and the other left.

⁴² "Therefore keep watch, because you do not know on what day your Lord will come. ⁴³ But understand this: If the owner of the house had known at what time of night the thief was coming, he would have kept watch and would not have let his house be broken into. ⁴⁴ So you also must be ready, because the Son of Man will come at an hour when you do not expect him.

⁴⁵ "Who then is the faithful and wise servant, whom the master has put in charge of the servants in his household to give them their food at the proper time? ⁴⁶ It will be good for that servant whose master finds him doing so when he returns. ⁴⁷ Truly I tell you, he will put him in charge of all his possessions. ⁴⁸ But suppose that servant is wicked and says to himself, 'My master is staying away a long time,' ⁴⁹ and he then begins to beat his fellow servants and to eat and drink with drunkards. ⁵⁰ The master of that servant will come on a day when he does not expect him and at an hour he is not aware of. ⁵¹ He will cut him to pieces and assign him a place with the hypocrites, where there will be weeping and gnashing of teeth.

NEW KING JAMES VERSION

³² "Now learn this parable from the fig tree: When its branch has already become tender and puts forth leaves, you know that summer is near. ³³ So you also, when you see all these things, know that it is near—at the doors! ³⁴ Assuredly, I say to you, this generation will by no means pass away till all these things take place. ³⁵ Heaven and earth will pass away, but My words will by no means pass away.

[36] "But of that day and hour no one knows, not even the angels of heaven, but My Father only. [37] But as the days of Noah were, so also will the coming of the Son of Man be. [38] For as in the days before the flood, they were eating and drinking, marrying and giving in marriage, until the day that Noah entered the ark, [39] and did not know until the flood came and took them all away, so also will the coming of the Son of Man be. [40] Then two men will be in the field: one will be taken and the other left. [41] Two women will be grinding at the mill: one will be taken and the other left. [42] Watch therefore, for you do not know what hour your Lord is coming. [43] But know this, that if the master of the house had known what hour the thief would come, he would have watched and not allowed his house to be broken into. [44] Therefore you also be ready, for the Son of Man is coming at an hour you do not expect.

[45] "Who then is a faithful and wise servant, whom his master made ruler over his household, to give them food in due season? [46] Blessed is that servant whom his master, when he comes, will find so doing. [47] Assuredly, I say to you that he will make him ruler over all his goods. [48] But if that evil servant says in his heart, 'My master is delaying his coming,' [49] and begins to beat his fellow servants, and to eat and drink with the drunkards, [50] the master of that servant will come on a day when he is not looking for him and at an hour that he is not aware of, [51] and will cut him in two and appoint him his portion with the hypocrites. There shall be weeping and gnashing of teeth.

EXPLORATION

1. What particular lesson from the fig tree did Jesus want his disciples to understand?

2. What did Jesus say about the timing of his return?

3. What was Jesus' point in bringing up the story of Noah?

4. Why did Jesus say his followers needed to watch for his return?

5. What is the point of Jesus' story about the faithful and wise servants?

6. What stern warning did Jesus give at the end of this parable to those who want to live as though he will never return?

INSPIRATION

As Jesus sought for a way to explain his return, he hearkened back to the flood of Noah. Parallels are obvious. A message of judgment was proclaimed then. It is proclaimed still. People didn't listen then. They refuse to listen today. Noah was sent to save the faithful. Christ was sent to do the same. A flood of water came then. A flood of fire will come next. Noah built a safe place out of wood. Jesus made a safe place with the cross. Those who believed hid in the ark. Those who believe are hidden in Christ.

Most important, what God did in Noah's generation, he will do at Christ's return. He will pronounce a universal, irreversible judgment. A judgment in which grace is revealed, rewards are unveiled, and the impenitent are punished. As you read the story of Noah, you won't find the word *judgment*. But you will find ample evidence of one.

The era of Noah was a sad one. "Now the earth was corrupt in God's sight and was full of violence" (Genesis 6:11). Such rebellion broke the heart of God. "His heart was deeply troubled" (verse 6). He sent a flood, a mighty purging flood, upon the earth. The skies rained for forty days. "The water rose so much that even the highest mountains under the sky were covered by it. It continued to rise until it was more than twenty feet above the mountains" (Genesis 7:19–20 NCV). Only Noah, his family, and the animals on the ark escaped.

Everyone else perished. God didn't slam the gavel on the bench, but he did close the door of the ark. According to Jesus, "That is how it will be at the coming of the Son of Man" (Matthew 24:39). And so a judgment was rendered.

Talk about a thought that stirs anxiety! Just the term *judgment day* conjures up images of tiny people at the base of a huge bench. On the top of the bench is a book and behind the bench is God and from God comes a voice of judgment—Guilty! *Gulp.* We are supposed to encourage each other with these words? How can the judgment stir anything except panic?

For the unprepared, it can't. But for the follower of Jesus who understands the judgment—the hour is not to be dreaded. In fact, once we understand it, we can anticipate it. (From *When Christ Comes* by Max Lucado.)

REACTION

7. One of the key elements of the "last days" will be the reality of judgment. Believers will be assessed at the judgment seat of Christ for the purpose of receiving rewards (see 2 Corinthians 5:10). Unbelievers will be judged at the Great White Throne (see Revelation 20). What is your honest reaction to this biblical fact?

_____

_____

_____

8. How much effort do you think believers should expend trying to figure out the sequence of end-times events? Why?

_____

_____

_____

9. What signs should we be looking for to know Christ's coming is near?

_____

_____

10. Do you think most believers truly live as though Christ could return at any moment? Do *you* live this way? Why or why not?

_____

_____

_____

11. How can we live in preparation for the at-any-moment return of Christ (see 1 Thessalonians 4:13–5:11 and 1 John 2:28)?

_____

_____

_____

12. What are some activities in your life right now that, in light of eternity, are probably pretty pointless and a waste of time?

_____

_____

_____

LIFE LESSONS

The Old Testament writers predicted the first coming of Christ. In every case, their prophecies were fulfilled to the letter. Likewise, the New Testament documents contain explicit details about the second coming of Christ. Why should we doubt the veracity of these predictions? The implications for us are clear. If Christ is returning ,and if his arrival is imminent, how are we living? Do our values and actions square with this ultimate reality? Or are we so focused on this life right now that we are forgetting the life just ahead? Either we heed and believe the promises of Christ, or we regard them as misguided and/or deceptive. There is no other choice.

DEVOTION

Lord Jesus, while I do not know all the details of your coming, I know the fact of it. You will return to earth. I believe your promises. Therefore, I need to be ready. As I read and reflect on your Word, renew my mind. Give me an eternal perspective that can help me avoid getting caught up in insignificant and worldly affairs.

JOURNALING

What are some of your unanswered questions about the "end times"?

_____

_____

_____

_____

_____

_____

_____

_____

_____

_____

_____

_____

_____

_____

_____

_____

_____

_____

_____

_____

_____

_____

_____

_____

_____

_____

_____

_____

FOR FURTHER READING

To complete the book of Matthew during this twelve-part study, read Matthew 24:1–25:46. For more Bible passages on the return of Christ, read Mark 13:1–23; Luke 12:35–40; 1 Corinthians 15:50–57; Titus 2:11–13; and Revelation 19.

LESSON TWELVE

HE'S ALIVE!

"Do not be afraid, for I know that you are looking for Jesus, who was crucified. He is not here; he has risen, just as he said."
MATTHEW 28:5–6

REFLECTION

Easter Sunday is the day on which Christians worldwide commemorate the resurrection of Jesus from the dead. However, for many Easter has become a mere holiday, the significance of which has obscured by secular hype. What was Easter like in your home when you were growing up? What traditions or customs did you observe?

SITUATION

Jesus had led an extraordinary life, filled with revolutionary teachings and jaw-dropping miracles, but it had ended with a horrific death on the cross. Only that wasn't the end. Matthew, like all the Gospel writers, concluded his account of the Carpenter-turned-King by demonstrating the authority of Jesus Christ over death itself. Matthew ends with a Messiah who is very much alive . . . and eager for the whole world to know it.

OBSERVATION

Read Matthew 28:1–10 from the New International Version or the New King James Version.

NEW INTERNATIONAL VERSION

[1] After the Sabbath, at dawn on the first day of the week, Mary Magdalene and the other Mary went to look at the tomb.

[2] There was a violent earthquake, for an angel of the Lord came down from heaven and, going to the tomb, rolled back the stone and sat on it. [3] His appearance was like lightning, and his clothes were white as

snow. [4] The guards were so afraid of him that they shook and became like dead men.

[5] The angel said to the women, "Do not be afraid, for I know that you are looking for Jesus, who was crucified. [6] He is not here; he has risen, just as he said. Come and see the place where he lay. [7] Then go quickly and tell his disciples: 'He has risen from the dead and is going ahead of you into Galilee. There you will see him.' Now I have told you."

[8] So the women hurried away from the tomb, afraid yet filled with joy, and ran to tell his disciples. [9] Suddenly Jesus met them. "Greetings," he said. They came to him, clasped his feet and worshiped him. [10] Then Jesus said to them, "Do not be afraid. Go and tell my brothers to go to Galilee; there they will see him."

NEW KING JAMES VERSION

[1] Now after the Sabbath, as the first day of the week began to dawn, Mary Magdalene and the other Mary came to see the tomb. [2] And behold, there was a great earthquake; for an angel of the Lord descended from heaven, and came and rolled back the stone from the door, and sat on it. [3] His countenance was like lightning, and his clothing as white as snow. [4] And the guards shook for fear of him, and became like dead men.

[5] But the angel answered and said to the women, "Do not be afraid, for I know that you seek Jesus who was crucified. [6] He is not here; for He is risen, as He said. Come, see the place where the Lord lay. [7] And go quickly and tell His disciples that He is risen from the dead, and indeed He is going before you into Galilee; there you will see Him. Behold, I have told you."

[8] So they went out quickly from the tomb with fear and great joy, and ran to bring His disciples word.

[9] And as they went to tell His disciples, behold, Jesus met them, saying, "Rejoice!" So they came and held Him by the feet and worshiped Him. [10] Then Jesus said to them, "Do not be afraid. Go and tell My brethren to go to Galilee, and there they will see Me."

EXPLORATION

1. On what day did the women visit Christ's tomb?

2. What specific supernatural events does Matthew say took place on that first Easter morning?

3. Whom did the women meet? What did he say?

4. How does Matthew describe the mood of the women?

5. What transpired as the women left to find the other followers of Jesus?

6. What specific instructions did the women receive in each of these encounters?

INSPIRATION

The empty tomb never resists honest investigation. A lobotomy is not a prerequisite of discipleship. Following Christ demands faith, but not blind faith. "Come and see," the angel invites. Shall we?

Take a look at the vacated tomb. Did you know the opponents of Christ never challenged its vacancy? No Pharisee or Roman soldier ever led a contingent back to the burial site and declared, "The angel was wrong. The body is here. It was all a rumor."

They would have if they could have. Within weeks disciples occupied every Jerusalem street corner, announcing a risen Christ. What quicker way for the enemies of the church to shut them up than to produce a cold and lifeless body? Display the cadaver, and Christianity is stillborn. But they had no cadaver to display.

Helps explain the Jerusalem revival. When the apostles argued for the empty tomb, the people looked to the Pharisees for a rebuttal. But they had none to give. As A.M. Fairbairn put it long ago, "The silence of the Jews is as eloquent as the speech of the Christians!"

Speaking of the Christians, remember the followers' fear at the crucifixion? They ran. Scared as cats in a dog pound. Peter cursed Christ at the fire. Emmaus-bound disciples bemoaned the death of Christ on the trail. After the crucifixion, "the disciples were meeting behind locked doors because they were afraid of the Jewish leaders" (John 20:19 NLT).

These guys were so chicken we could call the Upper Room a henhouse.

But fast-forward forty days. Bankrupt traitors have become a force of life-changing fury. Peter is preaching in the very precinct where Christ was arrested. Followers of Christ defy the enemies of Christ. Whip them and they'll worship. Lock them up and they'll launch a jailhouse ministry. As bold after the Resurrection as they were cowardly before it.

Explanation:

Greed? They made no money.

Power? They gave all the credit to Christ.

Popularity? Most were killed for their beliefs.

Only one explanation remains—a resurrected Christ and his Holy Spirit. The courage of these men and women was forged in the fire of the empty tomb. The disciples did not dream up a resurrection. The Resurrection fired up the disciples. Have doubts about the empty tomb? Come and see the disciples. (From *Next Door Savior* by Max Lucado.)

REACTION

7. Do you agree that there is no other compelling explanation for the radical change among the disciples except that they must have seen the resurrected Christ? Explain.

_____

_____

_____

_____

8. In the first century, Jewish women would not have been regarded as credible witnesses. How does this fact lend authenticity to the claim that two women were the first to see Christ alive?

_____

_____

_____

_____

9. Shortly after the events in this passage, the Jewish leaders and Roman guards concocted a plot to deny the story of a resurrected Christ (see Matthew 28:11–15). Why was their story so obviously false?

_____

_____

_____

_____

10. Matthew writes that some of Jesus' followers (and *some* would seem to indicate at least three) struggled with doubt—even though he was right there! In what ways do you find it difficult to trust in Christ?

11. If Christ was able to raise others from the dead, and if he himself conquered death, what are the implications for us as his followers?

12. What final promise do we read that Jesus made to his followers in Matthew 28:20?

LIFE LESSONS

Matthew's Gospel, from start to finish, is filled with gloriously good news. *Immanuel . . .* God with us. The sinless one, impervious to Satan's temptations. The messiah-king who offers citizenship in the now and not-yet kingdom of God. The compassionate healer. The ingenious teacher. The almighty miracle-worker. The Lord of the Sabbath. The enemy of false religion. The Son of David. The crucified Savior. The resurrected Lord who possesses all authority in heaven and on earth. The returning Son of Man. Christ is all these things and more. This is our message. *He* is our message!

DEVOTION

Father, thank you for sending your Son. What an incredible gift, and what an extraordinary life he led on this earth! By his death and resurrection, Jesus is more than able to save me from the penalty and power of sin. Now, may the Spirit of the living Christ reign in me, giving me the power to live as you command.

JOURNALING

What is the most significant insight you will take away from this study of the life, death, and resurrection of Christ?

_____

_____

_____

_____

_____

_____

_____

_____

_____

FOR FURTHER READING

To complete the book of Matthew during this twelve-part study, read Matthew 26:1–28:20. For more Bible passages on Christ's (and our) victory over death, read Psalm 23:4; Hosea 13:14; Romans 8:2; 1 Corinthians 15:54–57; and Ephesians 2:4–5.

LEADER'S GUIDE FOR SMALL GROUPS

Thank you for your willingness to lead a group through *Life Lessons from Matthew*. The rewards of being a leader are different from those of participating, and we hope you find your own walk with Jesus deepened by this experience. During the twelve lessons in this study, you will guide your group through selected passages in Matthew and explore the key themes of the Gospel. There are several elements in this leader's guide that will help you as you structure your study and reflection time, so be sure to follow along and take advantage of each one.

BEFORE YOU BEGIN

Before your first meeting, make sure the group members have their own copy of the *Life Lessons from Matthew* study guide so they can follow along and have their answers written out ahead of time. Alternately, you can hand out the guides at your first meeting and give the group some time to look over the material and ask any preliminary questions. Be sure to send a sheet around the room during that first meeting and have the members write down their name, phone number, and email address so you can keep in touch with them during the week.

There are several ways to structure the duration of the study. You can choose to cover each lesson individually for a total of twelve weeks of discussion, or you can combine two lessons together per week for a total of six weeks of discussion. You can also choose to have the group members read just the selected passages of Scripture given in each lesson, or they can cover the entire book of Matthew by reading the material listed in the "For Further Reading" section at the end of each lesson. The following table illustrates these options:

Twelve-Week Format

Week	Lessons Covered	Simplified Reading	Expanded Reading
1	God with Skin On	Matthew 1:18–2:12	Matthew 1:1–2:23
2	Overcoming Temptation	Matthew 3:13–4:11	Matthew 3:1–4:25
3	Power in Prayer	Matthew 6:5–15	Matthew 5:1–7:29
4	The Compassion of Christ	Matthew 9:18–38	Matthew 8:1–9:38
5	Following Christ	Matthew 10:24–42	Matthew 10:1–42
6	Heaven's Great Invitation	Matthew 11:16–30	Matthew 11:1–12:50
7	Spiritual Receptivity	Matthew 13:3–23	Matthew 13:1–52
8	Bread of Life	Matthew 14:6–21	Matthew 13:53–17:27
9	Humility	Matthew 18:1–14	Matthew 18:1–35
10	Missing the Messiah	Matthew 21:1–17	Matthew 19:1–23:39
11	The Last Days	Matthew 24:32–51	Matthew 24:1–25:46
12	He's Alive!	Matthew 28:1–10	Matthew 26:1–28:20

Six-Week Format

Week	Lessons Covered	Simplified Reading	Expanded Reading
1	God with Skin On / Overcoming Temptation	Matthew 1:18–2:12; 3:13–4:11	Matthew 1:1–4:25
2	Power in Prayer / The Compassion of Christ	Matthew 6:5–15; 9:18–38	Matthew 5:1–9:38
3	Following Christ / Heaven's Great Invitation	Matthew 10:24–42; 11:16–30	Matthew 10:1–12:50
4	Spiritual Receptivity / Bread of Life	Matthew 13:3–23; 14:6–21	Matthew 13:1–17:27
5	Humility / Missing the Messiah	Matthew 18:1–14; 21:1–17	Matthew 18:1–23:39
6	The Last Days / He's Alive!	Matthew 24:32–51; 28:1–10	Matthew 24:1–28:20

Generally, the ideal size you will want for the group is between eight to ten people, which ensures everyone will have enough time to participate in discussions. If you have more people, you might want to break up the main group into smaller subgroups. Encourage those who show up at the first meeting to commit to attending the duration of the study, as this will help the group members get to know each other, create stability for the group, and help you know how to prepare each week.

Each of the lessons begins with a brief reflection that highlights the theme you will be discussing that week. As you begin your group time, have the group members briefly respond to the opening question to get them thinking about the topic at hand. Some people may want to tell a long story in response to one of these questions, but the goal is to keep the answers brief. Ideally, you want everyone in the group to get a chance to answer, so try to keep the responses to just a few minutes. If you have more talkative group members, say up front that everyone needs to limit his or her answer to two minutes.

Give the group members a chance to answer, but tell them to feel free to pass if they wish. With the rest of the study, it's generally not a good idea to have everyone answer every question—a free-flowing discussion is more desirable. But with the opening reflection question, you can go around the circle. Encourage shy people to share, but don't force them.

Before your first meeting, let the group members know how the lessons are broken down. During your group discussion time the members will be will be drawing on the answers they wrote to the Exploration and Reaction sections, so encourage them to always complete these ahead of time. Also invite them to bring any questions and insights they uncovered while reading to your next meeting, especially if they had a breakthrough moment or if they didn't understand something they read.

WEEKLY PREPARATION

As the leader, there are a few things you should do to prepare for each meeting:

- *Read through the lesson.* This will help you to become familiar with the content and know how to structure the discussion times.
- *Decide which questions you want to discuss.* Depending on how you structure your group time, you may not be able to cover every question. So select the questions ahead of time that you absolutely want the group to explore.
- *Be familiar with the questions you want to discuss.* When the group meets you'll be watching the clock, so you want to make sure you are familiar with the Bible study questions you have selected. You can then spend time in the passage again when the group meets. In this way, you'll ensure you have the passage more deeply in your mind than your group members.
- *Pray for your group.* Pray for your group members throughout the week and ask God to lead them as they study his Word.
- *Bring extra supplies to your meeting.* The members should bring their own pens for writing notes, but it's a good idea to have extras available for those who forget. You may also want to bring paper and additional Bibles.

Note that in many cases there will no one "right" answer to the question. Answers will vary, especially when the group members are being asked to share their personal experiences.

STRUCTURING THE DISCUSSION TIME

You will need to determine with your group how long you want to meet each week so you can plan your time accordingly. Generally, most groups like to meet for either sixty minutes or ninety minutes, so you could use one of the following schedules:

Section	60 Minutes	90 Minutes
WELCOME (members arrive and get settled)	5 minutes	10 minutes
REFLECTION (discuss the opening question for the lesson)	10 minutes	15 minutes
DISCUSSION (discuss the Bible study questions in the Exploration and Reaction sections)	35 minutes	50 minutes
PRAYER/CLOSING (pray together as a group and dismiss)	10 minutes	15 minutes

As the group leader, it is up to you to keep track of the time and keep things moving along according to your schedule. You might want to set a timer for each segment so both you and the group members know when your time is up. (Note that there are some good phone apps for timers that play a gentle chime or other pleasant sound instead of a disruptive noise.) Don't feel pressured to cover every question you have selected if the group has a good discussion going. Again, it's not necessary to go around the circle and make everyone share.

Don't be concerned if the group members are silent or slow to share. People are often quiet when they are pulling together their ideas, and this might be a new experience for them. Just ask a question and let it hang in the air until someone shares. You can then say, "Thank you. What about others? What came to you when you reflected on the passage?"

GROUP DYNAMICS

Leading a group through *Life Lessons from Matthew* will prove to be highly rewarding both to you and your group members—but that doesn't mean you will not encounter any challenges along the way! Discussions can get off track. Group members may not be sensitive to the needs and ideas of others. Some might worry they will be expected to talk about matters that make them feel awkward. Others may express comments that result in disagreements. To help ease this strain on you and the group, consider the following ground rules:

- When someone raises a question or comment that is off the main topic, suggest you deal with it another time, or, if you feel led to go in that direction, let the group know you will be spending some time discussing it.
- If someone asks a question you don't know how to answer, admit it and move on. At your discretion, feel free to invite group members to comment on questions that call for personal experience.
- If you find one or two people are dominating the discussion time, direct a few questions to others in the group. Outside the main group time, ask the more dominating members to help you draw out the quieter ones. Work to make them a part of the solution instead of the problem.
- When a disagreement occurs, encourage the group members to process the matter in love. Encourage those on opposite sides to restate what they heard the other side say about the matter, and then invite each side to evaluate if that perception is accurate. Lead the group in examining other Scriptures related to the topic and look for common ground.

When any of these issues arise, encourage your group members to follow the words from the Bible: "Love one another" (John 13:34), "If it is possible, as far as it depends on you, live at peace with everyone" (Romans 12:18), and, "Be quick to listen, slow to speak and slow to become angry" (James 1:19).

Thank you again for taking the time to lead your group. May God reward your efforts and dedication and make your time together in this study fruitful for his kingdom.

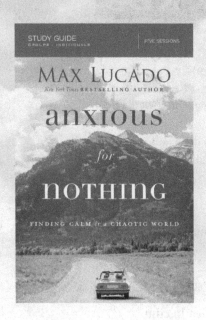
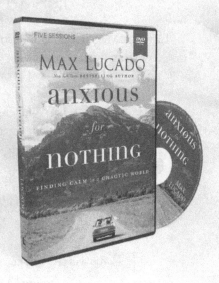

Sursell Comfy
Orthotic Sandals

support@sursell.
com

CPSIA information can be obtained
at www.ICGtesting.com
Printed in the USA
LVHW030704100222
709626LV00005B/27